BoR

Please renew or return items by the date
shown on your receipt

www.hertsdirect.org/libraries

Renewals and   0300 123 4049
enquiries:

Textphone for hearing   0300 123 4041
or speech impaired

D1427898

First published 2010 by Elliott and Thompson Limited
27 John Street, London WC1N 2BX
www.eandtbooks.com

ISBN: 978-1-9087-3976-6

9 8 7 6 5 4 3 2 1

A CIP catalogue record for this book is available from
the British Library.

Printed in the UK by TJ International
Typeset by EnvyDesign Ltd.

CONTENTS

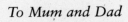

To Mum and Dad

ACKNOWLEDGEMENTS

Many people made invaluable contributions to this book, both to the original edition and to this updated version. In particular I would like to thank Geordie, David and George for their insights, Will, Alastair and Charles for their editorial assistance, Giles for his forbearance, Hubert, Jasper and George for kindling the fire of ambition, Lorne Forsyth and the team at Elliott & Thompson for making this happen, Mum, Dad and Charlotte for their endless support and Valentina for taking sales and marketing assistance to the most wonderful lengths.

INTRODUCTION

THINK THE WORLD OF FINANCE has nothing to
do with you? Think again. What might appear to be a
remote but corrupt oasis of privilege is in fact a giant oak
tree that towers over the global economy, affecting each
and every one of us. Whether shaping corporate strategy,
managing pension pots or raising capital for companies
and helping them grow, how the City fares has a direct
impact on savings, house prices, job prospects and the
prosperity of businesses across the world, from travel
agencies in Melbourne to hairdressing salons in Mumbai
and shoe shops in Madrid. As recent history has shown
us, when the City catches a cold we all start sneezing.

The last few years may not have been fun, but reports
of the industry's demise are premature. Writing off the
City has long been a popular pastime – no obituary has
been penned more often or with greater enthusiasm – but
history has shown the industry to be resilient and
resourceful, specialising in bouncing back from calamity.
The twentieth century alone saw two world wars and
major market crashes in 1929 and 1987, but each time
the industry's response was to stand up, dust itself down
and move on. There's no reason to believe it should be
any different this time. For all the talk of credit crunch
and the extra regulation, fewer jobs and lower pay that

will follow, the world of finance will one day emerge from the gloom.

It has to, for all our sakes. Our political masters know it better than anyone. Bashing bankers and their bonuses may have become a national sport in many countries, but look closely and you'll find that retribution hasn't always matched the rhetoric. The financial services sector is the heartbeat of the global economy. Strangling it would mean jeopardising billions of dollars' worth of tax revenue and many billions more of associated economic and social benefits. In London alone, each City job is reckoned to support four additional jobs.

Finance is a people business, pure and simple, and people are the focus of this book. Across the world millions work in the industry every day, and attempts to characterise each and every one as unscrupulous gluttons are as wide of the mark as assertions that bankers and their brethren are all innocent pawns at the mercy of a despotic few. The City has its fair share of both saints and sinners, all of whom contribute to an ever-bubbling cauldron of intrigue, subterfuge, petty jealousies and personal agendas.

To an outsider, City practices can seem arcane, but peel away the layers of jargon and self-importance and you'll soon find yourself transported back to the world of the playground. Many of the products and instruments the industry deals in are hugely sophisticated, but most of its methods and all of its mood swings are familiar to every single one of us.

In this book we reveal the industry and its people for who they are. We explain what stockbrokers, traders, analysts, fund managers and investment bankers do and how and why they do it, focusing on the tricks they employ and the webs they weave as they race each other to the top of the professional tree. Whether you aspire to work there and want to find out what really goes on, have been ensconced there for years and fancy a look in the mirror, or simply desire to learn the truth about a world so publicly vilified, this book provides a light-hearted, objective and accessible insight into the City, its people and its machinations.

If the events of the last few years have taught us anything, it is this: that for all the hand-on-heart conviction and repeated pronouncements, few people in the world of finance have any real idea of what is going on. It's not only stockbrokers, investment bankers and fund managers who are at a loss. Finance Ministers, Prime Ministers, Presidents and regulators are just as clueless.

In their helplessness they lurch from one extreme to another. Yesterday they favoured debt and today they're crying out for cash. The oil price is either too high or too low. Inflation and deflation each take turns to masquerade as the devil.

The market is the cruellest of mistresses. Compliant one minute and vicious the next, she chews you up and spits you out the moment you think you've mastered her. If success equated to second-guessing the market then most people would be stuck in the slow lane.

But finance is a game, a baffling, grown-up game admittedly, but a game nonetheless. The people who go furthest aren't always those with the keenest insights, the greatest skills or the finest qualifications, but those who understand the system and how to exploit it. Appearances can often be more rewarding than reality.

This book is about people, the ways they interact and their never-ending thirst for one-upmanship. It's about the game and how to play it. In the City, strange as it may sound, more often than not it's the psychologists and not the economists who hit the high notes.

AUTHOR'S NOTE

When I first wrote this book my intention was to describe life in the City – London's financial district, also known as the Square Mile – because that's what I knew about. However from researching the book and talking to colleagues and readers it's clear that its content applies more widely to financial centres around the world, from New York to Paris, Tokyo to Frankfurt. The names might be different but the roles are essentially the same. I have therefore given the book a new subtitle to reflect this but have retained references to the City in the text – to stand for the wider global industry – to avoid any unwieldiness.

Investment banks might trade everything and anything, from government debt to coconut oil, but to make things simple we'll concentrate on the instrument with which people are most familiar – namely stocks (or 'cash equities') – and bring in the other asset classes where relevant. Ultimately the selling, trading, analytical, investment and advisory processes are more or less the same whether you trade stocks, bonds, currencies, derivatives, heating oil or orange juice.

Alex Buchanan
April 2013

— 1 —

STOCKBROKING *OR* EQUITY SALES

'I'm now convinced that the worst thing a man can do with a telephone, without breaking the law, is to call someone he doesn't know and try to sell that person something he doesn't want.'

— MICHAEL LEWIS, *Liar's Poker*

PICTURE THE SCENE. It's six o'clock in the morning. You've already been up for an hour and are now sitting slumped on the train surrounded by the flotsam and jetsam of humanity. Everything is still, lifeless even. The strip lights flicker and then cough their fluorescent glow over puffy eyes, sagging skin and double chins.

Sounds awful, doesn't it? Welcome to the world of high finance.

In a Nutshell

Stockbrokers (or 'equity salesmen' or 'brokers') sell investment advice to professional investors ('fund managers' or 'clients') in return for commission. While servicing the client will involve certain ancillary duties that we'll explore later in this chapter, the commission that you generate is the yardstick by which you are judged. In essence, your job is to tell investors which shares to buy or sell and get them to trade these shares through your firm in return for commission.

The Early Bird Catches the Worm

Most stockbrokers arrive at the office anywhere between 6am and 7.30am GMT. This is an uncivilised hour at the best of times, but one that is particularly grim on a bleak morning in February. Those who live far from the office can expect to hear the alarm go off as early as 4am.

Now that's not funny, is it?

Sadly you don't have much of a choice. European stock markets open at 8am and brokers, traders, analysts and fund managers must all arrive early enough to prepare for the day ahead.

Exactly what time you arrive will depend on your own ambitions or on the guidelines set by your firm, but it invariably follows that the more ambitious you are or the more aggressive your firm is then the earlier you will arrive. How you get to work is up to you – some take the underground or bus, others drive scooters and a handful take taxis (but these tend to be either the *crème de la crème* or the habitually late). Some use the journey to read the *Financial Times* or *Wall Street Journal* or will catch up on sleep. You'll soon get used to the early mornings – everyone has to – but most nights you'll be tucked up in bed long before others in less exacting jobs have even considered leaving the pub.

In the larger broking firms the trading (dealing) floor is the size of a football pitch and holds hundreds of people. Brokers, traders (we'll discuss what they do in due course, see *Trading*) and a vast array of support staff sit crammed together like hens in a battery farm, floundering in a sea of screens, telephones and (misplaced) egotism.

Back to School

Many brokers don't have time for breakfast at home and so eat at their desks. An amusing game is to look up from your cereal bowl and see which of your colleagues is late for work. Salesmen who turn up late (this might mean arriving at 6.01am) will try to slip into their seats unnoticed, but more often than not will run the traditional gauntlet of disapproval from their more punctual colleagues. A late arrival will cause lips to be pursed and heads to be shaken. It's true – people really are this childish. In some firms those who arrive after the appointed hour are forced to buy lunch for the entire team (although not at a venue of the laggard's choice).

In terms of pettiness the average trading floor is no different from the average classroom. Substitute the teacher for the Head of Equities/Sales and the pupils for the brokers/traders and it's a close-run thing. It's all about denigrating the weak and sucking up to the person in authority.

AS IN ALL other City jobs, a hangover is not an excuse to be late for, or skive off from, a day's work on the trading floor. Honour demands that you arrive on time no matter how little sleep you've had or how much you've drunk the night before. You'll soon get used to sitting slumped at your desk and wishing the world would end. Look around the room on a Friday morning and see how many others are in a similar predicament.

Morning Glory

Most firms hold a meeting at around 7–7.30am GMT. This is the time when research analysts update the salesmen on any relevant stories (companies tend to make statements first thing in the morning) or on new research published on their stocks that day. In the larger firms you will stay at your desk while the analysts speak to the dealing floor over a microphone, while in the smaller houses salesmen and analysts are herded into the same room. You must then note down what the analysts say.

Some brokers will write down nothing at all. These individuals think either a) that they know it all already, or b) that the firm's analysts are useless and so should be ignored or c) that there's no point writing anything down because they stopped caring years ago. Don't be under any illusions – indifference, feigned or otherwise, is all part of the act. Watch as they lean back in their chairs, roll their eyes and yawn ever so conspicuously.

$

THE FINANCIAL WORLD IS full of people with God complexes. It's easy to spot a self-styled big hitter – most follow the same behavioural code. They suck up to their superiors, disparage or flatter their rivals (some enemies are best kept closer than friends) and ignore the rest of the world altogether, behaving as a king might in front of his courtiers. If a young broker comes to their attention it's because he's either very good or very bad at his job.

What you note down is up to you – it depends on what you think your different clients will want to hear. Much of what the analysts say might seem unremarkable or even irrelevant, but brokers can afford to put up their feet and put down their pens only when sure of their status.

Here's an abbreviated example of the sort of thing an analyst might say:

'This morning we have Q2 numbers from Martin and Wellbourne. Revenue was in line with expectations but EBIT was 5% short of consensus forecasts as discounting took its toll on the gross margin. EPS was 8% light thanks to the higher tax charge. Going forward the company expects the positive trend in like-for-like sales growth to be maintained. Early indications are that Q3 like-for-likes have been in the region of 2%. We[1] maintain our full-year forecasts and our outperform recommendation, believing that on 7x EV/EBITDA the stock looks good value versus the peer group.'

And here's another:

'You'll find on your desks a report we published last night on Automobiles de France. We maintain our in-line recommendation. Despite our conviction that the sector [industry group] has turned something of a corner, we feel this has been fully discounted by the market. Susan and I will be laying out our arguments in greater detail at midday today.'

What this actually means will be fully explained in a later chapter (see *Equity Research*). In the City there's much to learn in terms of jargon, and any new recruits are soon whisked off to the nearest classroom and indoctrinated in the *lingua franca* of the financial world.

When the morning meeting comes to an end most salesmen will pick up the phone and begin to call their clients (indeed, some might be making calls well before

---

1 Note the repetition of the first person plural. In the City people feel their arguments carry greater weight if couched in terms of collective responsibility.

the meeting has even finished). Only the very successful or
the very disillusioned will get up from their desks at this
stage, the former to stand and flex their muscles in true
Master of the Universe style and the latter to wander off
to the lavatories where they'll sit in contemplative gloom.

$

> IN THIS INDUSTRY success does not always correlate with
> intelligence nor disillusion with a lack of it. Ultimately it all
> comes down to what extent different people care about
> money or status, or both. Individuals with idealistic sensi-
> bilities will quite readily abandon these for the sake of
> acquiring a larger house or climbing another rung on the
> promotional ladder. We'll return to this theme time and
> time again, but in the City if you don't care then you'll
> struggle to succeed.

What You Say and Do

Most mornings will be spent contacting your clients either
by telephone, email or Bloomberg (see opposite) and
telling them what you think they might want to hear.

In theory brokers phone clients in order to give them
investment advice. In return they will expect to receive
'orders'. An order is when an investor buys or sells a
stock through his broker's firm. Commission is earned
by charging the investor a tiny percentage of the value of
the order. Orders can range anywhere from the tiny
($5,000) to the gigantic ($30m+) – it all depends on how
much money the client has and how much he trusts you
or your firm.

Trading stock is a not simple process. It is, in fact, a political
minefield. Never mind the actual mechanics of the buying
or selling (or 'dealing' – see *Trading*), in most firms more

than one salesman speaks to the same fund management house, and so it is often unclear which salesman generated the order. The picture becomes further blurred when one takes into account the armies of analysts and traders who have their own contacts with the institution in question. In this industry there are many snouts in the trough – apportioning credit where it is due is never straightforward. Learning how to grab the credit (especially when you don't deserve it) is the canny broker's greatest trick.

In reality brokers will look for any number of excuses to phone their clients – for appearances' sake they must be seen to be on the phone as often as possible. Investors tend to encourage this frequency of contact, not necessarily because they set any store by brokers' opinions but because they regard them as indispensable shoulders to cry on in times of trouble (of which there are many: a fund manager is the ultimate masochist – see *Fund Management*).

BLOOMBERG IS THE financial world's most extensive and expensive research tool, without which most City jobs would be considerably harder. At an individual cost of several thousand US dollars a month brokers, traders, analysts and fund managers can access information on practically any subject they choose, from stock prices and company information to sports news, restaurant reviews and adverts for cars and property (people will happily sell Ferraris or luxury apartments to each other via their Bloomberg terminals – there's no better proof of credit worthiness than a Bloomberg account!). Management never stop complaining about the cost and are always threatening to replace the system with something cheaper, especially when times are tough. However, not having your own Bloomberg terminal can be something of a social slur – it alerts both colleagues and clients to your (relative) insignificance.

In this job the most important maxim is 'know your client'. The good broker wears many different hats – he is psychologist, detective, agony aunt, nursemaid, administrator, entertainer, information filter and investment adviser all rolled into one. It matters not so much what you say (some investors will have forgotten a conversation as soon as they put down the telephone) as how you say it. If your tone is compelling and your manner is sympathetic then you soon become a drug they cannot do without. This world, like so many others, is all about trust. Convince a client you have his best interests at heart and you're up and running. The City's penchant for 'relationship building' is what keeps so many cocktail waiters, restaurant owners and wine merchants in business.

Let's have a look at some of the things you might say and do.

a) Call the client and repeat verbatim the morning meeting.

Reading from the sheet is the preserve of the unimaginative, the uninspired or the terminally depressed. It is the City equivalent of the human speaking clock or the actor who stands on stage and reads his lines from a script.

It's also what many brokers do. It's the easy option.

There is one catch, however. If all you do is read from the sheet, you may find yourself in a tight spot when your client wishes to dig a little deeper.

Much of what is said in your morning meeting will be repeated in other morning meetings in other broking houses the length and breadth of the City. If we take the earlier example, the response to the Martin and Wellbourne financial performance, we can safely assume that yours won't be the only broking house able to offer an opinion on this well-known company. Furthermore, if the investor cares about the stock and is any more than vaguely competent, he will have already interpreted the figures for himself (which the company will have made publicly available at 7am that morning).

Therefore when he wants a little more information and asks you,

'How does the valuation compare with that of the rest of the sector?'

Or,

'What like-for-like sales growth do you have pencilled in for the second half?'

Or,

'What is the present value of the lease commitments going forward?'

You'll need to be on your toes. What you do next is up to you. You can either a) look up the answer on your firm's comprehensive intranet, b) tell the client you'll get back to him or c) bluff.

Bluffing requires the least effort and is hence the most common response. The world of finance is built on bluff and counter-bluff.

Generally speaking, however, brokers get away with it when they read from the sheet. You'll be lucky to elicit as much as a grunt from an investor when you phone him early in the morning. In fact most fund managers with any sense don't answer their office phones before 11am. Some are still in bed while others are screening their calls, unwilling to encourage brokers they don't like, don't know or don't rate.

$

> THE LESS INTELLIGENT the fund manager is the more likely he is to ask you searching questions. It makes him feel important and his existence that little bit more relevant.

b) Call the investor and give your own interpretation of the morning meeting.

You don't always have to agree with your colleagues in Research. In most firms you'll be encouraged to deviate from the company line if it makes good commercial sense. Moreover analysts often get it wrong and, as we'll explore (see *Equity Research*), will sometimes say what they don't believe.

Let's use the Martin and Wellbourne example again. Here's what the analyst said,

'This morning we have Q2 numbers from Martin and Wellbourne. Revenue was in line with expectations but EBIT was 5% short of consensus forecasts as discounting took its toll on the gross margin. EPS was 8% light thanks to the higher tax charge. Going forward the company expects the positive trend in like-for-like sales growth to be maintained. Early indications are that Q3 like-for-likes have been in the region of 2%. We maintain our full-year forecasts and our outperform recommendation, believing that on 7x EV/EBITDA the stock looks good value versus the peer group.'

And here's what you might say (after you've dispensed with the small talk),

'I thought the M&W numbers were pretty uninspiring. The analyst thinks it's cheap and he's probably right, but I can't see the market getting too excited.'

At this juncture the client might agree and that will be it, and you'll move on to another subject, or he might say something along the lines of,

'Everyone's behind the curve. They're trading really well and margins are going to surprise everyone on the upside.'

What happens next? You are either

1) on top of your game and ready to debate all day long the whys and wherefores of Martin and Wellbourne without resorting to help from an analyst. It's safe to say many brokers will not be so well prepared.

or

2) unsure as to whether or not the client is right but ready to offer your support. You might make some spurious remark such as 'I think you've got a point there' or 'it makes sense – all the analysts have thrown in the towel'. You're now hoping he gives you an order to buy shares in Martin and Wellbourne.

Most phone calls don't translate directly into orders. Fund managers receive a barrage of ideas on a daily basis, a large number of which they consign to the dustbin. If an idea you come up with happens to fit in with the way they are thinking then they may well act on it immediately, but more often than not they'll go away and do their homework before forming a view. How much homework an investor does depends on the individual. Some will spend days or even weeks poring over facts and figures while others will quite literally flip coins or throw darts at a board.

It's not uncommon for a broker to phone an investor with an idea and for the investor to turn round and do exactly the opposite. What is more common is that you come up with one idea and the investor asks you to trade in a totally separate stock, or that he trades through your firm without you having phoned him first. What counts is how you and your firm service the client over the course of the year and not on a particular day.

What can also happen (and imagine how galling this can be) is that you give an investor an idea and he goes and executes the order through another broker. He doesn't necessarily do this to be perverse – the flood of information is such that he might easily forget which brokers gave him which ideas. A more common occurrence is that your client won't be responsible for the actual buying or selling of stocks but will delegate the process to a dedicated colleague or 'dealer' (see *Trading*). The dealer will have some (often too much) discretion as to with whom and how often he trades and should know which stocks to trade with which firms. Some firms will be more capable in certain names (stocks) than others, especially if that name is regarded as illiquid (hard to trade).

c) Call or email the client and tell him something relevant (ie about a stock/issue he has been following).

Let's assume that you know a particular client has an interest in Martin and Wellbourne. You might say,

'I'm hearing that M&W is going to surprise us all in Q4.

The analysts have all low-balled their estimates so the stock could easily squeeze from here.'[2]

And he might reply,

'That's what the bulls want you to think. It's going to get worse before it gets better. I'm a seller at these levels.'

Or he might say,

'Thanks – I've been hearing that too. I think I'll increase my position [buy some more stock].'

The point is that every conversation has limitless permutations. What should also be becoming apparent is that every person working in the industry is engaged in a game of educated guesswork, or just plain old bluff. No one – neither you nor the analyst nor the investor – knows the truth, but you're all employed (and very well paid) to guess what it might be.

d) Call up the investor and give him a new investment idea.

Analysts tend to be reactive (as opposed to proactive) and so much of what they peddle is their reaction to a company's announcement. Investors will lament that analysts rarely come up with any decent ideas, and this isn't totally unfair. We'll have more on this in a later chapter (see *Equity Research*), but much of the time analysts are involved in games of political football and are not encouraged to speak their minds. There are other issues too – equity research is a crowded field with many firms chasing the same ball.

2 Don't worry about the jargon at this stage. All you've told him is that the analyst community can't get any more depressed than they are already. If the company comes out with better than expected news then the share price is likely to rise.

As a consequence, originality is a rare commodity. Most ideas are rehashed versions of old ones – sheep in wolves' clothing as it were – and go round and round the City until everyone is converted to the cause (cf before prices crashed in the summer of 2008 every single investor seemed to own shares in the mining sector). At this point the only way for a stock is down – there are no buyers left to push up the price. As a broker you can filch your ideas from anywhere – analyst, client or even the tabloid press – and it's all about the presentation. While it's likely that the client will have seen the idea before, he may not have seen it from your particular angle.

Therefore, as a broker you'll be doing well if you come up with more than two or three genuinely good ideas a year. Whether or not the client takes any notice of you is another matter entirely. If you ring him and say,

'By the way, have you looked at the mining sector recently? Everyone assumes that China is going to grow by 10% next year but I think that's crap. All the analysts are smoking something. We should be selling these stocks.'

The client might reply,

'Yes, that's a very sensible idea. I think I'll sell my BHP [one of the world's largest mining companies].'

Or he might brush you off with,

'You're probably right, but I can't do anything today. It's the end of the month and I've got a whole load of reports to write.'

Or,

'Thanks, but I know that already.'

Or even,

'I don't agree. Iron ore pricing is going in only one direction and that's up. There's still a huge supply constraint.'

Sod's law dictates that if you're right and the client does nothing he won't thank you for the idea. It's also more than likely that if you're right and he follows your advice he'll think it was his own idea and will pat himself on the back.

But what do you think happens if you're wrong?

Yes, of course, it's your fault! He'll either say,

'Thank God I didn't touch that stupid idea of yours! It was obviously a disaster waiting to happen.'

Or he'll ring you up and berate you with,

'Why did you ever get me in to that piece of shit? Get me out NOW!'

GERMAN AND AMERICAN fund managers are quick to express their displeasure when things go wrong. Perhaps it's a cultural thing, but they feel quite comfortable savaging those who do their bidding. The English, by contrast, are less direct. They prefer to make sly digs or slag you off behind your back.

Get it wrong too many times and the investor will cut you off, however influential or important your firm might happen to be. But the beauty of the industry is this: no matter how dire your advice you can never be pursued for professional negligence. Compare this to a profession such as medicine, where you only have to sneeze before lawyers appear on your doorstep.

This is the reality of investment – it's a subjective not an objective exercise. Whatever fund managers might like to believe, they're nothing but speculators, educated speculators admittedly, but speculators nonetheless. If they get it right 60% of the time then they consider they're doing well, and that means if you as a broker achieve something similar then you're doing well too. If we're to believe John Maynard Keynes, the good investor should not be afraid to speculate. In his capacity as Bursar for King's College, Cambridge, Keynes wrote in 1938 that 'a speculator is one who runs risks of which he is aware and an investor is one who runs risks of which he is unaware'.

$

> WHERE FINANCIAL MARKETS are concerned, investors receive different layers of protection depending on the depth and breadth of their expertise. Professional investors are well aware of the risks involved and receive little or no protection. Private individuals, on the other hand, are not and hence have greater legal recourse if things go wrong. Most stockbrokers/equity salesmen deal only with professional (or 'institutional') investors. If your firm handles private client or 'retail' money then this will be dealt with by your colleagues in Private Wealth Management.

Investment ideas go in and out of favour with the passing of the seasons. In 2007 'cash' was a dirty word – fund managers and analysts alike pressed companies to hand it back to investors rather than save it for a rainy day. Bankers fell over themselves to lend money that companies could then pass on to shareholders. Fast forward several years and the picture had become quite different. No bank had any money to lend and companies were crying out for cash, especially those who had given it all away.

e) Call the investor and confirm something he already believes.

This is an obvious and common tactic and one that seldom fails. If you know an investor already happens to be thinking a certain way then telling him something that strengthens his conviction is only going to endear you to him. For the sake of commerce, brokers can be the most shameless sycophants.

'I think I remember you telling me that you're positive on the brewers? Well, we've just written a note [research report] on Heineken and the analyst says it's a screaming buy. It looks like you're one step ahead of him.'

f) Call the investor up about something unrelated to the stock market.

This might mean thanking him for an order, proposing meeting for dinner or enquiring how his son fared in the school rugby match or how his wife's appointment with the specialist went. In other words you'll look for any pretext to get him on the phone. At the end of the day the investor–broker relationship is all about pulling the right social and personal levers. You get to know him, get him to trust you and, hey presto, he'll be doing business with you. How much you tell him that's of any professional worth can soon become a secondary consideration.

$

IT USED TO be the case that if you knew the investor well enough to call him on his mobile phone then you should always try to, but in recent years the authorities have grown wise to this tactic. Calling a fund manager on his mobile or sending him a text is sometimes the only way to get hold of him – most don't have the time or inclination to answer their landlines or open more than a handful of the hundreds of emails they receive each day – and so you have to track him down to the one place he cannot hide. Every time he answers you or returns your call you take one step further into his socio-professional inner sanctum, something that can be only to the benefit of your future business relationship.

Broking firms have banned mobile phones on the dealing floor for some time, but only since regulators across the world started clamping down on insider dealing and other financial misdemeanours did they come clean as to the reasons why. Firms used to claim that mobile phones emitted signals that forced trading systems to shut down, but the reality was that information of a sensitive nature could be communicated without the authorities being able to intercept it. Fixed line calls and emails, by contrast, were never a problem – for many years now they've been recorded, preserved and scrutinised by compliance departments (in financial services what you say over the telephone is legally binding – you shouldn't promise a client something you can't deliver). As the market reached its zenith in 2007, too many brokers knew things they shouldn't (and that their clients would love to know), and some bad apples couldn't resist flying too close to the wind. If you happened to be taking a mid-morning stroll you might have seen any number of your colleagues out pacing the streets with mobile phones clamped to their ears. It's pure speculation, of course, but they can't all have been talking to their wives.

Rumour and mobile phones went hand in hand. Calling someone on their mobile from your mobile gave the impression you might know something you shouldn't.

'Hey, just thought you should know the rumour. I'm hearing British Telecom is going to get a bid approach on Monday.'

'Thanks. That's extremely interesting.'

More often than not British Telecom didn't get a bid approach on Monday. You were just passing on the same worthless rumour someone had told you in an attempt to appear well informed. Whatever the reality a client would often thank you for it – some people love a bit of intrigue.

The authorities, drowning in a torrent of post-credit-crunch criticism, hit back. All personal mobile phone use for work calls was to stop. Instead employees were to be issued with company-approved handsets, all of which would contain recording software (which in turn prevented many from actually working). But how effective this will be is anyone's guess. If someone has something to say and wants to evade detection his own phone is never too far away.[3]

CITY WORKERS AND their practices are policed by a combination of a) internal compliance departments and b) regulatory bodies such as the Financial Services Authority (or 'FSA') in the UK and the Securities and Exchange Commission (or 'SEC') in the US. Compliance departments, typically staffed by taciturn types with legal or accounting experience, delight in making life miserable for their more wayward colleagues (there is very little about compliance

3 How seriously he'll be taken is another matter entirely. In recent years corporate deal flow and rumoured bid activity has slowed to a trickle. The slump has been particularly marked in Europe – in May 2011 Barclays Capital reported that European M&A deal volumes were down by almost 250% from the 2007 peak.

that is humorous). Being asked to 'drop in for a chat' is often a prelude for a slap on the wrist or worse – Compliance never seem to need to see you unless you've done something wrong. Much of the time the crime will be petty in the extreme, such as you failing to sign a form or return a document, but on occasions you might have done something that could attract the attention of the authorities (such as saying something you shouldn't to someone you shouldn't). Firms like nothing less than to cross swords with the regulator. Even if one is proven innocent, a brush with the law only leads to publicity of the negative kind. If at all possible, wrongdoers will always be quietly removed rather than strung up in public.

The likes of the FSA and SEC exist, inter alia, to safeguard the stability of the financial system. Their failure to police the banks and their passion for risk (see Fund Management) in the run up to the credit crunch drew widespread criticism and in recent years they've taken pains to redress the balance, pursuing wrongdoers whatever their exalted status (the conviction in June 2012 of Rajat Gupta, former McKinsey Chief Executive and Goldman Sachs board member, for insider trading, conspiracy and securities fraud being one such example). While long overdue, turning the screw on regulated firms and their employees has only added to the malaise. As revenue-generating brokers, traders and bankers stuff their belongings into plastic bags and head for the exits so expensive recruits arrive in Compliance and unpack their clipboards and red pens. If ever there was a case of the tail wagging the dog then this is it.

g) Call the investor and tell him what everybody else is doing.

The world of fund management is becoming ever more transparent. Performance figures are made publicly available and investors, particularly those in the hedge-fund world, are able to compare and contrast their performance with those of their peers on a monthly, if not weekly, basis. Fund managers love knowing what their competitors are up to, particularly those whom they suspect are cleverer than they are. They'll happily sit around and discuss other people's performance for hours on end. If you phone an investor and tell him,

'Just thought you should know X has been building a position in Santander',

he'll always be grateful for the information. What happens next is up to him. If he thinks X is smart then he might follow suit. If he thinks X is an idiot then he'll give the matter no more attention and move on. If he regards X as his rival then he'll agonise over the issue for days, torn as to whether or not the other is right. If X is right and he follows him in then he'll congratulate himself on his foresight; if X is right and he does nothing then he'll curse X to high heaven, and if X is wrong and he does nothing then he'll jump for joy. What happens if X is wrong and he follows him in just doesn't bear thinking about.

Stocks will move on announcements that a certain investor has bought or sold a stake, and your clients will thank you for receiving this information before others do. Passing on such information before it's reported publicly contravenes the bounds of probity (if not the bounds of legality – the worst that can happen to you is a fine and removal from the City), and the authorities will crucify those they catch.[4]

---

4 There's a commercial reason as to why you should refrain from telling client A about what client B is up to. If you're indiscreet as to B's activities then A might very well wonder whether you're just as loose-tongued where his own activities are concerned.

h) Don't pick up the phone. You've got nothing useful to say. Do something else.

Having nothing useful to say is not an uncommon position for a broker to be in. When all hell's breaking loose, as can happen on occasion (eg throughout the whole of 2008), it's better to say nothing than ring up an investor and tell him something for the sake of it. But in firms where your client contact is closely monitored, this can be a courageous strategy. It can also be very tedious – you might sit there all day and have absolutely nothing to do. You'll just have to ask yourself: what price your professional integrity?

> SOME FIRMS ARE so paranoid that they monitor whom their employees do and don't call. If you don't complete your weekly quota of calls then you can expect to be hauled over the coals. What you said to your clients is of secondary importance – it's the fact you called that counts.

In truth, some brokers can't help themselves. They'd rather be on the phone talking crap and bluffing than be sitting at their desks twiddling their thumbs. And their clients aren't much better – they soon feel neglected if the phone doesn't ring, so they call their brokers and ask them why they haven't called. The whole thing's eerily reminiscent of an adolescent love affair.

> IF THEIR PERSONAL dealing accounts are anything to go by, fund managers might wonder why they take any notice of brokers at all. You might imagine that in addition to their pay packets brokers make a sizeable fortune from speculating in financial markets. After all, no one should be closer to the coalface. Unfortunately, the opposite seems to be true. Rather than parking money away in sensible long-

term investments, many of them can't resist the lure of the risky or the frivolous, and will gamble away small fortunes in stocks they know next to nothing about.

During the tech boom of 1999–2000, personal account ('PA') dealing exploded into life. Everyone from the Head of Equities down to the office tea boy dived in head first, not surprising if you consider that some firms went so far as to lend employees capital to make personal investments. Fund managers were no less rash, following their brokers into shares that no one knew the slightest thing about. This seemed destined to end in disaster, and often it did. One well-known broker blew up most of his client base when he persuaded them to buy into an obscure Swedish stock that he claimed would one day become the next Microsoft. When a client enquired what the company did and why he should buy it, the broker replied (somewhat testily), 'Oh I don't know, it's tech, just buy it!'

The fund manager took the bait, lost his shirt and refused ever to speak to the broker again. These days brokers and their brethren are far more circumspect when it comes to PA dealing. Stock markets have been too cruel for too long to tempt everyone lucky enough to have spare cash to shut their eyes and take the plunge. It's also far harder to do – compliance departments now impose so many restrictions on what you can buy or sell and when you can do so that for some people it's simply not worth the hassle.

Investors: All Creatures Great and Small

Right – so we've had a look at the sort of thing you might say, but what are the people on the other end of the telephone really like? Are fund managers all Hitler-types with incisive intellects, accountants who've forgotten how to smile or trainspotters with social consciences?

As you might expect, they represent the whole kaleidoscope of human nature – there's quite simply no such thing as the typical fund manager. You might imagine when you start out in the City that traders will be boisterous, brokers gregarious, analysts studious and so on, and while that generalisation is not too far wide of the mark, the longer you spend in the City the more diverse you will realise people are, even those who perform similar functions. Fund managers are an especially eclectic bunch. If anything can be said to unite them it is a passion for investing, but anyone who knows their fair share of them will have their doubts. Some fund managers claim to have no aptitude for investing and stay in the job only because they have a) no idea what else to do and b) no desire to wave goodbye to all that lovely money. We'll explore what makes a good (and bad) fund manager in due course (see *Fund Management*).

Personality is not the only differentiating factor. Fund managers invest in a variety of ways and have an array of styles, and just as dogs complement their owners so a broker should complement his client. You will hear terms such as 'hedge fund', 'prop trader', 'long-only' and 'private client' being bandied about. These are all different types of investor and salesmen will usually service one or sometimes two types of client. How these individuals invest and what they require from you is explored in other chapters, but you shouldn't assume that the oft-quoted stereotypes always apply (eg that all hedge-fund managers are aggressive and all private-client managers are soporific).

Callow Youth

In the early days no one takes the slightest notice of what you say. A fund manager will have more faith in his tealeaves or in his cat than in a fresh-faced graduate with a suit that doesn't fit. As a consequence you'll have plenty of time to practise what works and what doesn't. When you start out you will be allotted clients by your boss, but as you progress you will find them for yourself or they will find you. If you've been to the right school or university then you're already well set – you'll arrive on day one with a ready-made network of allies and advisers. The value of these contacts cannot be underestimated. While the City might like to consider itself a meritocracy, in no industry does the old school tie confer a greater advantage.

MOST BANKS CAN'T resist the lure of old-world royalty – an aristocratic title or two always looks good on the company notepaper. In one firm the head of sales was heard yelling across the dealing floor at a young Dutch broker, 'If your name was Schmidt you wouldn't even get a job in the buttery [company canteen]!'

As a young broker you will speak to the equivalent pipsqueak on the other side of the fence (eg your boss's client's junior) or to clients to whom no one else can be bothered to talk (because they have little or no money to invest). More often than not you will find the latter to be sympathetic characters who are only too delighted that someone has given them the time of day. If you screw things up with these clients your boss won't care. Junior fund managers know just as little as junior brokers and so won't notice your mistakes, while insignificant clients will either be too ignorant or too polite to say anything.

During the early days a lack of experience is your greatest impediment. If you ring up a client and tell him to buy a stock because your analyst loves it, he might very easily turn round and say,

'But, hang on a minute, management promised the same

things five years ago and look how they screwed up. Why should anything be different this time?'

And you will be stumped. Now, a lack of experience is not your fault and simply takes time to correct. Therefore, learn as much as you can as quickly as you can. If you need to ask stupid questions then go and ask them.

$

> IT'S HARDER TO get away with bluffing when you first arrive in the City. Your youth and inexperience mean that investors will scrutinise more closely what you say. Brokers of several years' standing, by contrast, will often behave in the most cavalier fashion. The Head of Sales at a leading broking firm once got himself into hot water when he rang up a client and advised him to sell a position in a FTSE 100 company. Much to his astonishment the client called him every name under the sun and hung up on him. Unfortunately the broker had forgotten that only an hour earlier he had telephoned the client's colleague and told him to increase his position in the same stock! A junior broker might not be so negligent.

There are some clients with whom, try as you might, you never succeed in establishing a rapport. You can spend much of the time wondering whether it's because you have or haven't done something or whether you have offended them in some way, but these characters are so uninspiring that they struggle to engage their wives or children, never mind the broking community. They're quite content to sit like dummies at one end of a telephone as brokers wonder why they bother on the other.

'Good morning, Frank. I hope you're well.'

'Hmmm.'

'Just got a few things to run you through if I may.'

Silence.

'Well, this morning's figures from L'Oréal went down well with our analyst. He thinks that…'

And after five minutes of monologue,

'…And that's all for today. Speak to you soon.'

'Hmmm.'

The worst clients are those who think they know everything – these are the real bastards. They'll take every opportunity to catch you out and you should phone them only if you have done your homework and/or are feeling heroic. Your boss will claim that these are the best clients because everyone else is too frightened to phone them, but this is a fallacy. They are unfriendly because they don't like you and there's no point rationalising why. In extreme cases a client will shout at you and curse your incompetence. You have no choice but to sit there and take it. The client is always right.

This is another instance where experience is invaluable. Young brokers take criticism to heart and find it difficult to stand up to angry clients, however unreasonable or overbearing their behaviour might be. Older brokers, on the other hand, are more adept at sidestepping criticism and will do their level best to hand over the more sadistic clients to those with less say in the matter.

A European fund manager, renowned for her bad temper, would change her hair colour to suit her mood. Brokers knew when to avoid her when she dyed her hair red – she would rant and rave and hang up the phone at the slightest provocation. Trying to be helpful was a dangerous tactic at the best of times. She was as likely to thank you (and give you a large order) as she was to slam down the phone and scream,

'Go fuck yourself! Why didn't you call me an hour ago?'

$

IT·DOESN'T HAPPEN often, admittedly, but on occasions you may just get to suckle at the teat of human kindness. One Korean fund manager was so desperate to do the right thing by his brokers that he would trade even when he didn't have to. Bemused by his behaviour, a broker once asked him why he was always willing to buy stocks and sell them for a loss a short time later. Was he lost in translation? The investor, far from revealing any sensational strategic or even fraudulent methodology, replied that it was all about being popular with his brokers. The more commission he paid them the happier they would be. If he lost money so be it.

It's a Jungle Out There

In later chapters we shall examine in some detail the roles and responsibilities of the other dealing-floor participants. For now it is worth concentrating on your relationship with the analysts and the traders. You will have daily contact with both and how they view you and your contribution is critical to your position in the political food chain.

As a broker you need to have both groups on your side – analysts because they provide you with ideas and can be wheeled out to see your clients as and when you require, and traders because they transact business with the client's firm. Aligning yourself with an intelligent analyst or with a trader who knows what he's doing or who is trusted by the client's dealer makes good commercial sense. It ensures that the flow of business between you and your client is appropriately regular.

Fund managers pay commission to broking firms for three main reasons: research, trading (or 'execution') and primary deal flow (we'll explore what this means in due course). This has led people to question the validity of the salesman and to predict his demise, but he continues to exist (and to matter) because he is a) the main conduit to the fund management community (who have all the money) and b) the social glue that binds every firm.

In recent years the financial world has become so much more liberated. Pre the Big Bang of 1986 – the name given to the establishment of a new modus operandi for the City of London – fund managers and traders had to liaise via brokers, they couldn't go direct. If any City protagonist has had to defend his ground and redefine his role since then, it's the broker. Technology has increasingly obviated the need for a middleman. These days everyone can, in theory, talk to everyone. In a world of 'experts', a broker is the classic minister without portfolio.

But the City is all about snobbery, inverted or otherwise, and snobberies take time to shift. Traders, analysts and fund managers will often refuse to communicate, sometimes for the most childish of reasons. As a rule, analysts still consider traders to be socially or academically inferior and will avoid certain fund managers; traders deride analysts for being geeks or idiots (especially if their ideas never make money); and fund managers are critical of both, dismissing traders as jumped-up market traders and analysts as overpaid plagiarists.

We could spend all day analysing why people fail to hit it off, but this is not the time. Instead, we can simplify things by observing that each party has his own agenda – traders are focused on market timing or 'feel', ie the best time to buy or sell a stock; analysts have longer-term horizons while, depending on their investment strategy, fund managers sit somewhere in the middle.

But they all condescend to talk to the broker. And, like the good diplomat you are, you keep each and every one of them sweet, getting it in the neck from one while placating the other.

> WITHIN EACH COMMUNITY you will have your favourites, either because you like them or because you think they're talking (relative) sense. But try not to make too many enemies – falling foul of an influential analyst or trader won't do you any favours. And expect to be treated like dirt when you first arrive – analysts and traders have the same contempt for young brokers as some others do for the women who drift in like ghosts and empty the bins at night. It's sad but true.

Red Tape

Like any threatened race, brokers were swift to recognise their vulnerability and to apply the appropriate remedies. Sitting astride the City's perceived social or intellectual fault lines could be turned to their advantage – they could become point men par excellence, packaging up the different services a broking firm offered and offering them to the investor in a presentation box. In this they were aided and abetted by management who, as we shall see, had their own reasons for wishing to encourage the survival of the species.

In recent years broking firms have become increasingly

obsessed with the culture of 'account management'. In its simplest form this translates as 'wringing the greatest possible amount of commission out of a particular client'. Each salesman is allotted a number of client accounts to manage, is set a commission target and is then forced to explain once or twice a year why actual commission is short of forecast commission (such targets are rarely, if ever, realistic). An account manager's role is not just about providing the client with a series of scintillating investment ideas. He also has to introduce the client to the right analysts and companies, and to ensure that his colleagues on the broking side are speaking to the corresponding individuals on the client's side.

Account managers will visit the client once or twice a year in order to conduct an 'account review'. On these occasions account managers will be accompanied by a member of management, typically the head of sales or head of research. These account reviews are akin to school reports. Every aspect of the various services – research, trading, corporate access and primary business – provided by your firm will be examined and evaluated by the client, and those present will discuss how service levels might be improved (resulting, of course, in increased commission). As a contributor to the account you must wait nervously for the report, hoping that your contribution has not only been acknowledged but also that it has been seen to have improved since the last review.

Large broking firms think they have a divine right to be paid, and if you work for one of the big boys then in some ways you have it easy. The variety and depth of the services you offer mean that investors cannot afford to ignore you. It is quite common for an investor to lament,

'We pay X or Y an obscene amount of commission but they never give us a good idea.'

In a big firm you will soon realise that the quality of your ideas can be an irrelevance. Fund managers allocate most of their commission pool to the big firms because they want access to the latter's trading capabilities (big firms are prepared effectively to subsidise their clients), primary business, corporate contacts and clever analysts.

In other words, even if you lose them money investors still have to pay you.

As a consequence, a broker in a large firm may soon wonder how much individual merit he really has. The answer, in all honesty, is not much. Most people, unless they are exceptional, are cogs in a highly efficient machine. If you disappear then someone steps in to replace you. It's as simple as that.

In small firms the individual matters so much more. Investors won't talk to you unless they feel they really have to, and even then you can spend months giving a client the most brilliant ideas and he won't pay you a penny. In many ways those working for the big boys have it easy – much of the time business comes through the door in spite of and not because of you or your efforts. On the other hand, what small firms lack in professionalism or efficiency they tend to make up for in terms of camaraderie and community spirit. The staff of one small firm used to spend their Friday afternoons sunning themselves in the garden of the local pub. Sometimes things got so slack that the chief executive was the only one left on the dealing floor. He'd stand at the window and glower until someone noticed and alerted the rest to his presence. They'd then all troop back in like naughty children, revelling in their rebellion.

COMMISSION LEVELS VARY and depend on the size of the client and the frequency with which they trade, but the top brokers can expect to receive $15m+ per annum from each of the leading hedge and pension funds. Recent years, however, have seen commissions heading the wrong way fast – in 2012 they ran at no more than 40–50% of their 2007 peak. Everyone was affected but the smaller firms disproportionately so – they had neither the scale nor the breadth of product to withstand the blow in the same way as the bigger boys.

The Competition

As a broker you will always be aware of your competitors, no matter how good you or your firm think you are. A stock will move as much on recommendations published by leading brokers as on announcements made by the company, and share prices can be buffeted in different directions as rival brokers indulge in private battles of wits. This is particularly significant if one or both firms has a proprietary position (ie has invested its own capital) in a stock – see *Equity Research* and/or *Fund Management*. Some brokers take particular pleasure in trashing the merits of a stock a rival has been pushing:

'Our friends down the road are talking out of their arses – there's no way that Automobiles de France is going to grow earnings [profits] by 20% next year. I'd be staying well away if I were you.'

THERE ARE A handful of mega brokers – Citigroup, Goldman Sachs, JP Morgan, UBS, Credit Suisse, Deutsche, Morgan Stanley, Bank of America/Merrill Lynch and Nomura – and then a whole medley of smaller fry, many of whom specialise either in certain territories or certain sectors. Some larger stocks will be covered by up to 30 or even 40 different houses.

Clients might ask you to give them preferential treatment in the form of the 'first call' (ie they get you to phone them before you phone anyone else), but if you don't get your skates on then you will find that a broker from a rival firm has already called and stolen your thunder. Speed can be of the essence. You don't want to phone a client and find that five other brokers have already called him on the same subject. The clever broker will either get his call in first or ensure that he finds a different subject to discuss from everyone else.

Investors tend to have no more than a handful of favourite brokers, and if you're included in the pantheon then it's likely that you'll be aware of who the others are. Their merits won't necessarily be similar to yours. Investors choose brokers for a wide variety of reasons – eg the best stock-picker, the best administrator, the best looking, etc.

> SOME BROKERS AND their clients even become the best of friends, happy to socialise without the need of the corporate Amex. One well-known fund manager and his broker regularly spend their Friday lunchtimes in the local cinema, rubbing shoulders with a ragbag of students, tourists and other skivers.

We have already seen how broking firms love administration – they also adore poring over league tables and reams of statistics. How your firm ranks compared to the peer group is to some a matter of life or death. There are various surveys (one of which is Extel, the City of London's equivalent of the Oscars) that go into the most extraordinary detail. Surveys are dangerous in that you can get penalised (in the form of remuneration) if your department performs badly but shouldn't expect the converse if it does well (but see *Equity Research* – it can be different for analysts). A good survey result serves only to justify a manager's existence and thus any benefits go into his and not into your pockets. Some of the more enlightened firms shun these surveys – they set greater store by profits than by league tables.

Certain firms are known for being strong in certain sectors, either because they have a well-regarded analyst or because they have valuable corporate relationships in that area. Clients will contact you for advice on subjects where you are perceived to have an edge (and will disregard your views where the opposite is believed to be true). However, being perceived to have an edge doesn't necessarily mean you do (and vice versa). Investors pay particular attention to brokers who are believed to enjoy close proximity to their corporate clients.

THE GREATEST COMPETITIVE threat may lurk a little closer to home. The dealing floor can be an intense place to be, particularly when egotism and testosterone are in abundance. Brokers and traders will compete to see who can get the largest orders and write (generate) the most commission – it's all about who's the biggest swinger in town.[5] Don't be surprised if the knives come out for you – in the City the knives are out for good and bad alike. You're either too arrogant or too laissez-faire – there's very rarely a grey area.

Coining it In

Discussing the merits or otherwise of quoted companies (those listed on a recognised market) with your clients is

---

5 We'll focus more on this in due course – see *Trading*. In most firms the live orders and/or commission figures are available on a daily basis and brokers will watch like hawks to see who is doing the business and who is languishing in the slow lane.

the bread and butter of a broker's existence, but where your firm really makes its money is in what is known as 'primary business'. Without going into the various specifics, primary business involves raising fresh capital for companies, listed or otherwise, and this is when you and your colleagues go cap in hand to the client base in search of the requisite cash.

A common type of primary deal is the IPO (Initial Public Offering) – this is when a company (or 'corporate client') sells (or 'lists') its shares on a given stock market, thereby soliciting a new group of shareholders. Stockbroking firms love these deals because they can be very lucrative – corporate clients pay many times the commission rates that fund managers are charged. Companies list on stock markets when they desire a) widespread access to capital b) a transparent value for their business (many companies incentivise employees by awarding stock that they can buy or sell) and c) the increased profile a stock market listing brings. If the business thrives and the share price rises, these new investors will benefit, making them more likely to back any future plans management might have.

City fees are obscene, especially where primary business is concerned. By way of example, if a company wants to raise $100m via the equity markets it will be charged anywhere between $3m and $7m for the privilege (and that's before it has paid off the lawyers and any other hangers-on). Broking firms are unwilling to undercut the competition for the sake of winning business – the fee system is a cartel in all but name. In any other industry (except perhaps private education) such behaviour would be outlawed for being anti-competitive.

By contrast, secondary market transactions – ie buying or selling a share that is already listed – cost a fund manager considerably less. Commission rates depend on the client but can range from 0.01% to 0.3% of the total transaction value.

In recent years IPOs have been increasingly thin on the ground, reflecting both risk aversion on the part of investors and reluctance from companies to commit to a process than can be anything from frustrating to brand-damaging (European IPO volumes totalled a mere $17bn in 2012, down from $128bn in 2007). Such reluctance is easy to understand when one considers how many high-profile companies have struggled to raise the requisite capital, seen their share price dive post-listing or failed to get the deal away at all. Whereas investors used to pull every favour they could in the rush to be allocated stock in the next must-have deal, these days they sit on the sidelines and do their best to pick holes in any company brave enough to test the water. Some even seem to take a vindictive pleasure in dismantling the dreams of the company, its shareholders and its bankers. This isn't so surprising when one stops to think about it – in these straitened times no one likes to be helping line somebody else's pockets.

The lack of IPO activity has had serious and long-lasting ramifications for a wide variety of parties, from companies looking for capital to investment banks/ broking firms/lawyers thirsty for fees to private equity funds keen to offload assets (for an insight into the private equity industry see *Corporate Finance*). For many years banks and broking firms structured their equity departments around the IPO goldmine, hiring legions of bankers, salesmen and analysts to cater for the expected influx of deals. In fact some firms ran secondary franchises at a loss safe in the knowledge that hefty IPO fees would ease them safe into bonus territory. But as IPOs have dried up and corporate work ground to a standstill so management has had to make tricky decisions – do they cut costs and axe staff or hold on and wait for the good times to return? This is a particularly pressing issue for smaller firms, much of whose very existence depends on the IPO machine and whose obituaries are penned with growing regularity.

Like so many other financial disciplines, 'running' an IPO is about a) process and b) politics (for a more detailed description of the IPO process and the politics behind it, see *Corporate Finance*). It's common for broking firms to team up when conducting an IPO, forming what is known as a 'syndicate'. The idea behind a syndicate is to showcase the company to as wide a range of potential investors as possible, and the more brokers you have on your side the wider you can cast the investor net. Syndicate membership is hierarchical, with the larger firms running the deal, advising the company as to price and structure, choosing who markets the stock to which investors (important brokers want to talk to important investors) and taking the lion's share of the fees. Small firms tend to take the process extremely seriously and do their utmost not to stand on the big boys' toes (if they want to be invited back to the next IPO party they'll make sure they behave themselves) – IPOs are a great chance to demonstrate professional competence, bag a fee and cock a snoop at the peer group. Don't imagine that this involves trying to raise more money than the guy down the road. More often than not fees are pre-agreed and performance is measured in terms of how many meetings your sales team can arrange. In other words, syndicate members compete to see which has the greatest capacity for administration.

For brokers and fund managers alike the IPO process is one big tactical battle of wits.

The broker can be forced to IPO (or 'float') companies that he wouldn't think of recommending to his worst enemy, but economic expediency (ie his bonus) demands that he closes his eyes and picks up the phone. His job is to get first his analyst (for what is known as 'pre-marketing' – see *Equity Research*) and then the company in front of as many investors as possible, and to persuade these investors to participate in the fundraising. Investors, on the other hand, will do their utmost to avoid these fundraisings and will invent any number of fantastical excuses as to the reasons why.

Some firms have the unfortunate habit of losing their clients' money in IPOs – quite simply their deals are never as good as they make them out to be. It is, however, harder than you might think for the investment community to run for the hills – in the City a strict policy of *quid pro quo* is in operation. Refusing to contribute money towards one IPO kitty can lead to the client being ostracised when a more attractive deal comes to town.

WHEN A DEAL is popular and everyone wants to be involved, someone will be left disappointed. You'll get used to clients ranting and raving when they receive less stock than they asked for. Divvying up stock is a political exercise and one that as a junior broker you have no say in whatsoever. As a rule the institutions that pay the most commission/support the most IPOs get the lion's share of the cake.[6]

One investor tactic is to wait until the last possible minute before making a decision on whether or not to participate. This way he gets to gauge the popularity of the deal – for fund managers as for analysts (see *Equity Research*), there's a safety in numbers. The more popular the deal the

6 See *Corporate Finance* – only senior members of a syndicate have any real say in how much stock an investor is allocated.

better the shares should theoretically perform once the company is listed (and vice versa). Some investors are not looking to hold the stock long term but to 'flip' it (sell it on within a few days/weeks) for a quick profit. If they think a deal is building up a head of steam then they will join the party just as a deal is closing. If demand for the shares isn't satisfied during the IPO process then the price should in theory move up once the company is listed and investors buy more stock in the 'after market'.

So if a client calls and asks you,

'How many times is the book covered?'

He wants to know whether or not it makes sense for him to subscribe. What you do next depends on how scrupulous you are. If the deal is popular then you'll say so. If, on the other hand, it isn't then you'll have to weigh up your options. You can either a) tell him the truth and hope that he subscribes anyway, or b) warn him off and risk the wrath of your boss or c) bend the truth in an attempt to lure him into the book. Many brokers choose to bend the truth – it's the easiest way of getting your boss off your back.

S

> INVESTORS ARE LIKE elephants – they never forget. Broking firms live and die by the quality (or otherwise) of the companies they help to promote. Having a reputation for losing your clients money in IPOs can be something of a millstone around your neck – fund managers don't like being conned any more than anyone else.

For each and every party, the IPO process is all about greed. Company and investors pull in different directions and your colleagues in equity capital markets (or 'ECM', the investment bankers who control the IPO process – see

Corporate Finance) run around like obsequious chickens in an attempt to keep everyone happy. As the salesman you are caught in the middle and will invariably get it in the neck – either the deal is over-priced/unappealing and you can't sell it or it's so 'hot' that there's a bun fight for stock. It's at times like these when you wonder whether you are nothing but a well-paid punch bag.

SOMETIMES YOUR FIRM will get deals away but only after something of a struggle – certain brokers are brilliant at pulling in favours at the eleventh hour. If you've got one of your clients to subscribe to an iffy deal you'll then spend the next few weeks staring at a sagging share price and praying that the client has better things to worry about.

Management can be unbearable when an IPO is on. They're constantly cracking the whip, chivvying and harrying you to ensure you're pulling your weight. When a deal goes live most brokers are ordered into work at an ungodly hour (6am is common) to prepare for the day ahead. Syndicate members agree a start time, and it's then up to the individual salesmen to see who can beat the competition and call their contacts first. Firms who play it straight will often wish they hadn't – others (especially the bigger boys) are quite happy to ride roughshod over what was, in theory, a gentleman's agreement. It's quite common to phone a client a minute after an IPO officially goes live and hear him say,

'But X called me on the subject ten minutes ago. I've already agreed to see their analyst.'

In the UK companies like to have their hands held and so employ what are known as 'corporate brokers'. What these corporate brokers do and why they exist is dealt with elsewhere (see *Corporate Finance*), but for now it will suffice to describe them as a company's eyes and ears around the markets, always ready to funnel feedback and comment back and forth between the company and the investment community.

On certain occasions a company will want to get an idea of what its shareholders are thinking and will engage its corporate brokers to find out. Members of the ECM department will then come and ask you and your colleagues on the sales desk to phone up the institutions that count and canvas their views.

On the flipside, fund managers will use corporate brokers to find out what a company is really up to and will pay special attention to individuals perceived to have the requisite clout with the company in question. Some of these people will command legendary status – a company and its shareholders will often want quite different things, and an ability to bridge the divide is a rare and valued gift. If you work for a firm with a renowned corporate broking franchise you will often be asked by your clients what this banker is saying about that company. Investors will dole out large sums of commission for this information, regardless of how valuable or otherwise they consider you and your research department to be.

Climbing the Management Ladder

We have already mentioned that, in the City, intelligence is no guarantee of success. Getting ahead is as much about political cunning as anything else. People who are on paper quite undeserving will often trample all over those who seem to have the world at their feet.

Brokers are divided up into teams according to the clients they service. If your clients are hedge funds then you'll be part of the hedge-fund sales team, and if they specialise in smaller companies then you'll be part of the smaller-companies team, and so on. How your unit functions depends so much on your personality and those of your colleagues. Teams who make too much noise (and hence seem to be having too much fun) will be frowned on by more sepulchral and/or self-important colleagues.

Let's now consider the type of person you might encounter in the typical broking firm. It goes without saying that this list is not exhaustive.

a) Mr Do-Gooder

He's destined for the upper branches of the management tree but will never reach the very top. He is reliable, industrious and uninspiring. He embraces every task with relish (he's the perfect account manager) and has absolute faith in the management creed, playing the straightest of political bats. Peers and subordinates alike will gather to stick barbs in his back.

b) Dr Jekyll and Mr Hyde

Bright, devious and politically astute, at heart he's a cold-blooded pragmatist. He exudes charm but will stop at nothing to get to the summit, happy to disparage friend and foe alike. He is both well informed and disingenuous; ultimately he acts in the firm's (ie his own) and not in his clients' best interests. Investors listen to what he says but learn to take it with a pinch of salt.

c) Mr Smile & Dial

Amenable, persistent and as politically minded as anyone, he's also, unfortunately, not very bright. His ideas will be set in stone until he changes his mind (which he'll do most afternoons, particularly if he's had a good lunch at his club). He likes to be seen to be busy and will be on the phone all day chewing the cud with his cronies and lunching buddies.

d) Mr Blue-Eyed Boy

This one has a lot to prove and can make your life a misery. He may have felt socially or academically disadvantaged when younger and will regard the City as his route to salvation. He likes diligence, dislikes frivolity and will refuse to fraternise at work. He's always first to spot the next investment trend, although it is never his fault when everything goes wrong. His drive and thirst for commission will lead him to the top of the tree, often at a very young age.

e) Mr Existential Angst

Mercurial, cynical and prone to indolence, he'll often attain management status but one day will crack, forcing his despairing superiors into deciding whether to sack or indulge him.

f) Mr Cigarettes & Alcohol

Brokers have any number of weaknesses and for some alcohol and drugs are never far away. Some find it difficult to say no, often those in positions of responsibility. He may have visited the last chance saloon on several occasions, but such is his clout with his clients that he always escapes the axe. This is just as well for his bank manager – he's either paying alimony or has squandered everything he ever earned.

g) Little Miss Sunshine

In what is still a man's world, a pretty face never goes

amiss, particularly if she has a nice smile and even nicer legs. Many married fund managers can't resist a female broker – as far as some of them are concerned her opinion on the market is an irrelevance, but she makes them feel so much better about life. Every broking firm should employ a Little Miss Sunshine – it's a commercial no-brainer.

CHAUVINISM IS ALIVE and well in the City. Women do hold prominent positions but they are few and far between, and while some may be lauded for the ability to juggle a demanding job with a multitude of children, people are quick to snipe and will soon resort to knowing looks and 'I told you so' comments when things go wrong.

In order to succeed, a woman must have a particular brand of resilience. Male managers are happy to hire them if they look good but only too willing to boot them out once they appear ready to run off and become mothers (perhaps one of the reasons why women earn less than men of comparable standing). It's no coincidence that more pregnant women were fired as the downturn deepened – hiding behind the alibi of firm-wide redundancy programmes was the only legitimate way their bosses had of purging them. Many men continue to remain suspicious of women in the workplace – a bank or broking firm hates nothing more than being slapped with a lawsuit for harassment or discrimination – and in some eyes this makes women a dangerous hire. As a consequence a woman must enter this industry with few illusions and with her eyes wide open. Whether she likes it or not everything about her will be that much more closely scrutinised.

---

h) Monsieur Vaudeville

Every broking firm does, however, employ a comedy European, in theory to pursue business opportunities overseas but in reality to allow the English/Americans respite from their own inadequacies. Whether he is French, Dutch, Swedish, German or Spanish, M Vaudeville is renowned for his eccentricities, terrible English and even more terrible clothes. He can be unfailingly polite or stark, raving mad (or both).

i) Mr Living Dead

We mentioned earlier the lure of the old school tie – Mr Living Dead belongs in the stockbroking graveyard but just refuses to die. He drones on all morning to his equally dreary clients, quoting passages from the *Daily Telegraph* or *Country Life*, and then spends the afternoon snoozing at his club or at his desk. Management can't stand him and look to boot him out at the earliest opportunity, but such is his resilience and the scope of his address book that sooner or later he pops up again at another firm.

Slowly but surely several things should be becoming apparent:

1) That many of those at the top of the management tree have no actual interest in managing. Ultimately they're political animals with one main concern – themselves. Let's not be too harsh – solipsism is not solely a broker's preserve – but you'll soon learn that your boss's interests do not always tally with yours. If you want to get ahead then you too must learn to play the political game.

2) That in order to succeed in this world you must have a thick skin. Those who don't all too quickly recoil from the atmosphere of self-importance and struggle to reconcile the paucity of the contribution with the enormity of the pay packets. They'd run away and become teachers if only they could afford to.

3) That pragmatism, contacts and political connivance will often get you further than flair and/or integrity. In the City there is little sympathy for the idealist.

> BROKERS ARE ALWAYS well represented in the highest echelons of management, not because they all make superior managers but because they know how to read the political tea leaves. The ethereal nature of the job means that they have a constant need to justify their own existences, and what better way to do this than to run the show?

At the Top of the Tree

Toe the line for long enough and you might just reach the rarefied environs of management. But for long before that fateful day you'll be at the mercy of your boss.

Bosses are an eclectic lot. They can be revenue-generating superstars, whip-cracking enthusiasts, sympathetic shoulders to cry on, middle-of-the-road plodders or administrators par excellence, but what they all have in common is a) political cunning and b) absolute faith in the company creed. Bosses care. Bosses sweat blood for the cause. And when times are tough – as when the credit crunch began to bite – they put aside personal enmity and stick together. After all, why sack each other when you can sack the staff?

Be warned – your boss can make your life a misery. He's not always there to be your friend or your confidant. If he's nodding sympathetically as you pour out your heart he's probably wondering how best to get rid of you. Keep your counsel, keep your head down and keep the commission rolling in. Bosses who truly care about your welfare are a luxury enjoyed by a minority.

Some bosses live in glass boxes at a safe distance from hoi polloi. On the rare occasions that they are a) in this office, b) not on the phone and c) not surrounded by furtive-looking cronies, they'll be squinting at their computer screen wondering why the numbers never add up and who might be the appropriate scapegoat. If you need to speak to them, you'll approach the box with caution, knock gently and just pray they remember who you are.

Other bosses are more hands on, sitting in and among their team on the dealing floor. If you're really unlucky he'll be sitting right next to you. He'll then notice every time you're away from your desk, how long you take for your lunch, how many personal calls you make and how often you surf the internet. It's better to have him safely tucked away in his box where he can't see you.

$

IT'S BEST NOT to socialise with the boss's family if you can avoid it. One broker met a girl in a nightclub, went back to her house and called in sick the following morning. Not appreciating that she still lived with her parents, he wandered down to breakfast at a leisurely hour in his underwear to find her father sitting at the table eating his cornflakes having also called in sick. To his horror he discovered that her father and his boss were one and the same!

Listening In

Most brokers and traders have on their desks that is known as a 'dealer board', a piece of kit which displays the different telephone lines used by members of your team. The dealer board is designed so that anyone can answer anyone else's phone (just in case a client is phoning to give an order – there are no answerphones in broker land) and so that everyone can be on the same call at the same time. This makes privacy an issue – you can be making the most personal of calls unaware that someone else has clicked into your line. Some brokers spend much of their working day drinking in the florid details of other people's private lives.

One broker used to have a beautiful but tempestuous girlfriend. She would call up several times a day (sometimes as many as fifteen) and berate him for the most trivial of misdemeanours. His colleagues always knew when she was on the phone – he would bury his head under the desk, speaking to his loved one in terse, urgent whispers. This was the cue for the rest of the team to click into the line, settle back and enjoy the show. Aware of what was afoot and all too fond of the spotlight, he would look to antagonise her, driving her fury to ever-greater crescendos for the sake of his audience.

Young brokers looking to get a sense for the job are encouraged to listen into the phone calls of their elders and betters. On one occasion a graduate tapped into a call just in time to hear a client ask his colleague,

'Just who was that idiot who picked up your phone this morning? He was absolutely bloody useless. I'd have him fired if I were you.'

And the broker replied,

'I couldn't agree more. We all think he's a total waste of time.'

Making the Coffee

The financial community adores arranging meetings, and as a stockbroker you will attend your fair share. Like clients, meetings come in different shapes and sizes, and you will soon realise that while you might attend many meetings, in very few will you make any meaningful contribution.

This is because you are a 'fixer'. In other words, you help put companies and analysts in front of investors, ensuring that the former gets to the right place at the right time. Some brokers suspect that they are nothing more than glorified travel agents/tour guides and, in truth, they're not far wrong. There can't be many other industries where highly qualified men and women have to sit in silence for hours on end listening to the conversations of others, occasionally leaning across the table to top up a water glass or coffee cup. You'll soon learn how different investors take their coffee or how to carry six plastic cups at the same time. If you need consoling just imagine how much less real waiters and waitresses are paid!

IF YOU ARE adept at/enjoy making small talk then you are at an immediate advantage. This is particularly relevant for brokers servicing clients in foreign countries, where you will have to escort companies from one investor meeting to another for what is called a 'road show'. Sitting in gridlocked traffic for hours on end can be testing even when faced with the most garrulous of company, but imagine what it's like when the corporate client is self-important, inappropriately flirtatious (more of a problem for female brokers) or downright miserable. You must grit your teeth and bear it. Corporate clients pay big fees and don't you forget it.

Sleeping or Star Gazing?

You don't always sit in meetings and say nothing. Sometimes companies come in and present to you and your colleagues, usually when they have something to announce (eg their yearly/half-yearly results or when they plan to buy another company). In both cases they are seeking investor approval and are using your firm as their PR department. On these occasions you have the opportunity to participate by asking intelligent and uncontroversial questions (usually from a script prepared by the sector analyst). Most young brokers keep quiet as they are frightened to ask anything stupid, while those older brokers vying for promotion/recognition compete with each other to see who can ask the most questions, scrambling over each other in the manner of eager schoolboys. One way for you to stay awake (you will find this difficult at 5pm if you've been in the office for over ten hours) is to check which of your colleagues are asleep. Watch their eyelids droop and then shut. After several seconds they will wake with a jolt, hoping that no one has seen them. Perhaps it's no surprise they fall asleep so easily – the financial calendar is nothing if not predictable. You'll soon get used to shaking the same hands (and hearing the same tired excuses) in the same weeks of each passing year.

Sometimes the companies that come in and present are household names (eg Volkswagen or Vodafone) and their management teams are no less celebrated. Having a ringside seat at the battle of wits between a tenacious broker and an even more tenacious Chief Executive is one of the highlights of the job. On other occasions you'll bury your head in your hands when a colleague, for the sake of being seen to be keen, asks something inane like,

'Do you have a progressive dividend policy?'

Or (even more embarrassing),

'I understand you own the Cosmic Coffee brand? Well,

I was in my local branch last Saturday and my wife thought the muffins were cold and stale.'

$

A MEETING WITH a tobacco company always used to be fun, not because management had anything interesting to say but because they persisted in promoting their wares, thereby flouting anti-smoking regulations. The do-gooders would wince and splutter as clouds of smoke chugged across the room. Only if you were really important would you be allowed to light up too.

Other meetings you'll attend will be with analysts, often when they have a new piece of research to present. These occasions are less deferential than your average company presentation, not least because some salesmen regard analysts with the same contempt they have for the man who sweeps the street or makes their cappuccino in the local cafe. On these occasions you might be tempted to ask a question, but avoid asking one that requires a long-winded answer at the end of the meeting (like elderly men, analysts will use 20 sentences where two will suffice). Most of your colleagues will be in a hurry to escape to nowhere in particular and won't thank you for it.

Keeping the Customer Sweet

If you insist on opening your mouth in meetings then you might consider accompanying investors to meetings both at home and abroad. This way you get to visit companies together and then discuss your findings afterwards. An investor will always be grateful for your input, particularly if he has had a late night and is crying out for inspiration.

Brokers and their clients often discover a common bond when out exploring the more prurient nightspots that a foreign city has to offer. Visiting companies is all about what the locals and not the company management have to offer. Being let loose, however, at the firm's expense can be too much for some people. Brokers, analysts and investors will sit slumped in meetings glassy-eyed and giggling, wearing their nocturnal endeavours like a badge of pride. At the end of the day, rabble-rousing and not research is the quickest way to an investor's heart.

Nothing better reflects economic reality than the financial world's attitude to client entertainment/employee expense accounts. When times are good management will give you carte blanche to take clients out on the town. There's nothing better than several bottles of wine or a guilty secret to bring the two of you closer together. Investors who never return your calls will become your new best friends once they recognise that you have virtues and/or vices in common. Some brokers spend much of their spare time holed up in restaurants, drinking dens and houses of ill repute. And for good reason – they'll be paid handsomely whatever they tell the client the following morning!

Prudent manipulation of your expense account can improve your quality of life no end. Fancy dinner at a glitzy restaurant? Take a client! Want to play golf? Take a client! Your wife has a passion for opera? Take a client (and his wife/mistress)! A fund manager will never say no – everyone loves a freebie, especially when it means an afternoon out of the office. And it's all above board. It's the return on investment that counts.

However when times are tough and the market is in freefall everything is very different. Brokers used to club class will slum it on budget airlines and swap the Four Seasons for something less salubrious, while investors will be reluctant to accept a broker's hospitality when there isn't sufficient commission to repay him. Furthermore management will go through your expenses with a toothcomb, doing their utmost to quibble over the most minuscule of claims.

'Are you sure it was a client you called? What could you have been discussing at that time of night?'

Or

'Did you really have to take a taxi to the airport that morning? What was wrong with the train?'

Since the credit crunch the authorities have jumped on the bandwagon, issuing strict guidelines for what can be given or received without it constituting bribery. Talk about the sheriff arriving in town long after the cowboys have cleared out!

IF YOU'RE GOING to spend money on a client, make sure you don't get landed with the bill. One broker was so keen to impress his clients that he managed to blow $50,000 in one night of excess! Management were incensed and insisted he refund the money. He claimed he couldn't and appealed for their understanding but his entreaties fell on deaf ears – they were adamant. The head of a rival firm, who had long wanted to hire the broker but had always been rebuffed, moved in. He'd pay the $50,000 debt in the form of a signing-on bonus but only if the broker switched firms. The broker had no choice but to accept.

Looking to the Future

Does your lack of specialisation count against you if you get sacked or want to jump ship and pursue opportunities in another professional field? This is a moot point. Many City workers are exposed in that they have no professional qualifications except those relating to finance – indeed some fret that, unlike their friends with accounting or legal backgrounds, they have no expertise to fall back on in times of trouble. Here brokers might feel somewhat vulnerable. While analysts, fund managers and corporate financiers at least have grounding in accounting and financial reporting, brokers, like traders, have only their wits and their address books to hang their hats on.

At the same time, wits and address books are not to be sniffed at. Selling is the key skill in any industry and some contacts can be worth their weight in gold – many brokers milk these contacts to go on to bigger and better things. Some even become successful fund managers. The reality is that if you're bright and/or resourceful you'll never be short of the right opportunities.

SOMETIMES YOU DON'T have to be either – you just have to be in the right place at the right time. One of the few hedge fund success stories of 2008 was sacked three years earlier by his broking firm and left to rot on the scrap heap. As his former boss lamented, 'I fired that bastard and made him four million quid last year!'

Leaving the Office

The early departure is the compensation for the early start. Most European stock markets close between 4 and 4.30pm GMT, and if no meeting is scheduled then most brokers will leave by 5.30pm (if you work for a firm that values face time then you might consider hanging around until 6–6.30pm). What you do is up to you but those looking to get ahead will speak to clients (some investors answer their phones only at certain times of day) or (pretend to) read research.

Another advantage of the job is that you are never required to work at the weekend. Unlike your friends in corporate finance, you can work as a broker and still enjoy a healthy social life. Your work is not project-based and thus your professional existence is tied to the hours that the market is open. At weekends you might choose to read the business sections of the Sunday broadsheets, but that's as far as it goes work-wise.

> BACK IN THE good old days (ie 2003–07), a broker might raid his firm's expense account and take his best clients away for the weekend – the Swiss Alps, the Hamptons and Ibiza were all popular destinations. To the chagrin of nightclub operators around the globe, the savaging of the hedge fund industry has put a stop to all the fun.

How and What You Get Paid

Historically most City jobs combined a basic salary with a discretionary bonus (payable in both cash and company stock), and stockbroking was no different. Basic salaries, even for senior management, were capped at around $200,000 to $300,000, and it was the discretionary element that determined whether or not you got rich.

Post the credit crunch, however, public indignation over bonuses and the City's anticipation as to the actions the authorities might take to limit the discretionary element of bankers' pay gave rise to a dramatic shift. Some firms front-loaded the remuneration of senior employees, driving basic salaries as high as $500,000 for Managing Directors in an attempt to ensure they retained key staff. Raising the 'fixed' element of compensation has had two major consequences, namely a) increasing the risk to a bank's shareholders (unlike bonuses fixed salaries are promised at the beginning of the year before the bank knows what's going to be in the pot) and b) forcing firms to shed middle-ranking employees in an attempt to balance the books. In 2012 one small broking firm cut so many staff that it had no one left to sell its products – management were certainly not going to stoop so low – and so had to hire new recruits at great expense.

CAPPING BONUS PAYMENTS has not been the only way the authorities have sought to curb what they regard as casino-style behaviour. Other measures have included subjecting bonuses to a) deferrals (ie spreading payments over a number of years) and b) claw backs (in the event of poor performance). All this might suggest that City remuneration will never again scale previous peaks but don't be surprised if it does – investment banks are nothing if not resourceful when it comes to bending the rules to suit themselves!

In most firms management do not use a mathematical formula to work out what to pay you – ie you do not take a fixed percentage of the commission you generate (much is the pity). Instead, individual department heads receive a pot that they must divide up among their team. This pot doesn't always equate to the profits that your department or you deliver – there can be a 'robbing Peter to pay Paul' element as money is shunted between departments and individuals. It is not uncommon for brokers to lament that their pay packets have been savaged by the poor performance of departments and colleagues that have nothing to do with you (and vice versa).

While commission is the yardstick by which you are judged, what you get paid from the pot doesn't necessarily correspond to the percentage of the departmental commission that you generate – working out that percentage is all but impossible. Despite the best efforts of broking firms to get their clients to split out how much they pay for the different sell-side services (so called because brokers, traders and analysts 'sell' ideas and services to fund managers, who are in turn known as the 'buy side'), no one seems any the wiser as to who does how much for whom – there are too many claims, counter-claims, crossed wires, knives in the back and snouts in the trough.

As a consequence, commission is an important factor in calculating your remuneration but is by no means the only one. Playing politics is just as vital. If you a) get on well with your colleagues (what traders, analysts and corporate financiers say about you matters), b) are seen to be diligent around the office (helping out with company meetings, IPOs and all the administration broking firms adore), c) have a rapport with your boss and d) appear to care (this is critical) then you'll be well set. In the City it all comes down to whether or not your face fits – this is why one man can generate 20 times the commission of another and still take home the same pay packet.

AS A RULE of thumb most people aren't paid anywhere near as much as you fear they are or as much as they would like you to believe they are. When times are tough your bonus (if you receive one) will contain a greater weighting of stock than during boom periods (although this will be of little consolation if your firm's share price is heading south – anyone from Lehman Brothers or Bear Stearns can confirm this), but even during the good years pay packets were skewed far more to stock than to cash.

> Awarding stock is one way of tying you in to your firm. Stock is generally subject to a 'lock-in' – this means that you cannot get your hands on it for a pre-agreed length of time (usually several years) and will forfeit it if you leave of your own volition before the prescribed date.

In essence, what you earn as a broker depends on your performance within the context of the departmental pot. It is therefore impossible to generalise, particularly in the context of the current environment, but in the average firm during an average year the average broker can take home a total package of anywhere between $150,000 and $450,000.

Now that's not bad, is it?

Conclusion

Mention the word 'stockbroker' and people have long been liable to get hot under the collar. Oscar Wilde, among others, considered them social pariahs, purveyors of hot air and not much else. As he wrote in *The Picture of Dorian Gray*, 'With an evening coat and a white tie, anybody, even a stockbroker, can gain a reputation for being civilised.' Today stockbrokers still have their critics. Some even consider that they run the sell side, enjoying a level of power quite disproportionate to the value they add.

The broker's demise has been long predicted, most often by people with axes to grind and/or smaller pay packets, but this is yet another City prediction that has run aground.

Brokers have always performed a vital role and will continue to do so (unless human nature undergoes a radical overhaul). Financial services, love it or loathe it, is a people business, and brokers are the glue that binds it. They sit in the middle of everyone (traders, analysts, corporate brokers and fund managers) and conduct the financial orchestra.

Don't be under any illusions – like so many others this job has its ups and downs. You'll have to stomach large dollops of drudgery, mediocrity and repetition, be ready to dodge any number of political bullets and meet pompous, self-important and over-promoted automata, ciphers for spouting other people's unqualified opinions. And yet sales desks can be fun, energising places where intelligent and amusing people abound. If you can close your eyes and accept it for what it is – a game – then you're already a step ahead. Sometimes it's better to join in than to carp from the sidelines.

Let's put it another way – how many other careers are there where you have little or no professional liability, are home in time for tea and can become a millionaire by the time you're 30?

— 2 —

TRADING *OR* DEALING

'"Wall Street," reads the sinister old gag, "is a street
with a river at one end and a graveyard at the other."
This is striking, but incomplete. It omits the
kindergarten in the middle.'

— FREDERICK SCHWED, JR,
Where Are The Customers' Yachts?

DEPENDING ON WHOM you ask, sales and trading go together either like Bonnie and Clyde or Cain and Abel. Spawned from the very same seed, they're either best friends or in a constant state of civil war.

Once upon a time sales was the preserve of the gentleman and trading that of the barrow boy, but these days the two are more adjacent than ever. Trading may be the more upwardly mobile – technological advances have transformed its reputation, and today's hot-shot graduates now seek to become traders instead of brokers – but class prejudices take time to shift. In many firms a trader, for all his commercial virtues, remains the salesman's social inferior.

But brokers and traders also have much in common – their jobs are closely related and they're prey to many of the same frustrations, temptations and aggravations.

Most of the issues we explored in the last chapter (such as client relationships, pay structures and internal politics, to name but three) we'll encounter here, so differences will be pointed out as and when they occur.

For traders, as for brokers, getting in a client's face is what counts. As long as you have something to say (however tenuous) and can change your mind on a moment's notice, then you should have no problem at all.

In a Nutshell

Trading (or 'dealing'), in its most basic form, is the buying and selling of different assets (shares, bonds, futures, options, currencies, commodities, etc) either for your firm or on behalf of an investor (or 'client'). Traders fall into several camps. On the sell side there are a) 'sales traders', b) 'dealers', c) 'market makers', and d) 'prop traders', and on the buy side there are 'dealers' (not to be confused with the sell-side function of the same name). As everyone treads on everyone else's toes (and those of brokers and fund managers), we'll try and keep things as simple as we can.

Once Upon a Time in London:
A History Lesson

Back in the 1980s the City of London looked like a very different place. Not only was it a fraction of its current size (in terms of both personnel and the sums of money involved), but the way in which business was transacted was also a world away from today's multi-faceted banks, high-tech dealing floors and real-time trading systems. Back then, if an investor wanted to place a trade, he'd make a call to one of the many firms dotted around the Square Mile and rouse a red-faced broker from that day's racing pages.

'Denning, old boy, I'm thinking of having a nibble at some Grand Met. Could you get me a price and size?[7]

The broker would then put down the phone, stub out his seventh cigarette of the morning and make a call on a radio to a dealer or 'yellow button' on the stock-exchange floor.

'Barry, be a good fellow and get me a price and size in Grand Met.'

'Yes, Mr Denning.'

The stock-exchange floor was a bear pit of a place, a mass of humanity where men of every size and shape would scream, shout and wave their hands and arms in every imaginable direction (a bit like a demented bookies' ring). There the yellow button would approach a 'pitch' (market stall), fight his way through the throng and ask the 'jobber' (market trader with terrible temper and/or acidic humour) for a price and size in Grand Metropolitan.

Jobbers were today's equivalent of market makers. They bought stock from X and sold (or 'jobbed') it on to Y for a profit (or 'turn') – that at least was the aim. Jobbers specialised in certain stocks and competed with jobbers from rival firms. They had a gift for working out which way the market was moving and set their prices accordingly. One sniff of the wind and they could tell whether a share price was heading up or coming down.

Dealers and jobbers were living legends and had nicknames to match. In a sea of a thousand faces, nicknames were used to

7 To put it another way, he was telling the broker that he wished to buy shares in Grand Metropolitan (which merged with Guinness in 1997 to form the modern day Diageo) and wanted to find out how much stock the market would sell him and at what price.

mark an individual out from the crowd. 'Jaws' (he'd eat you for breakfast), 'Hackney Gurkha' (he was short, dark and came from Hackney), 'Earl of Essex' (he was fond of large houses in Essex), 'Honest Jack' (he could never conceal whether he was buying or selling), 'Streaky' (he was as lithe as a streak of bacon) and 'Hosepipe' (he was well endowed and had a brother called 'Sprinkler') are all examples of famous nicknames. In those days everyone did business face to face. There was no such thing as anonymity.

To the request for a price and size the jobber might respond,

'I'll make you 34–6 in a 100.'

And the dealer would reply,

'Thank you very much, sir.'

In other words the jobber would sell 100,000 shares at 36 or buy 100,000 at 34. The spread – ie the difference between the sale price (or 'offer') and the purchase price (or 'bid') – was where he made his money.

A jobber didn't have to reveal his hand if he didn't want to. He could instead tell the dealer,

'I'll make you 34 in a 100.'

And not make it clear whether he was a buyer or seller. If the dealer pushed him to reveal his position or 'opened him up', then the former had to trade through him whatever the other prices being offered on the floor. Although the City still in part retains this philosophy, in those days *dictum meum pactum* or 'my word is my bond' was ingrained into every stock-market participant. As everyone knew everyone, you couldn't screw people over. It was too small a world.

If the dealer had discretion to act on behalf of the client he could deal at the price he was given or could visit another jobber and try to find a better one. If he didn't have discretion he'd get back on the radio and pass the price and size up to the broker, who would in turn call the fund manager and relay the information. If the client wanted to trade then the dealer would return to the jobber, the 'bargain' would be recorded in a ledger and the financial settlements made accordingly. Once upon a time there was no such thing as electronic cash transfer.

As we shall go on to explore, how the City works today is in essence not too dissimilar, at least from a human perspective. Technology has, however, shifted – and is continuing to shift – the goalposts, and the sheer size of the industry has engendered new roles and made others redundant. But ask any old-timer and he'll give you the same answer – back then the City was a more charismatic, more collegiate place.

Pre the Big Bang of 1986, no one had ever heard of electronic trading, fund managers couldn't talk direct to dealers or jobbers (they had to go via brokers), trading commissions were fixed and stockbroking outfits weren't allowed to be part of financial conglomerates (such as American banks). But the march of progress is relentless, and London's evolution from parochial bullring to global behemoth was always inevitable.

If anyone first saw the potential, it was the Americans. Here was a city that spoke (passable) English, sat flush on the Greenwich Meridian (meaning you could trade Tokyo for breakfast, London for lunch and New York for dinner), had an ardent capitalist for a Prime Minister in Margaret Thatcher and was not too stringent where regulation was concerned. The British welcomed their cash, technological innovations and working practices with open arms. It was a marriage made in financial heaven.

What Thatcher saw then, politicians see now. The financial services industry is the UK's golden goose – all other industries pale into the shade in comparison. No one was angrier than the political elite when the credit crunch erupted and bankers were caught sleeping at the wheel. In the electorate's eyes good deeds abroad(!) count for so much less than economic prosperity at home. As Mayor of London Boris Johnson put it at the 2009 Conservative Party conference, 'But never forget, all you would-be banker bashers, that the leper colony in the City of London produces 9% of UK GDP, 13% of value added [tax] and taxes that pay for roads and schools and hospitals across this country.'

These days there are fewer nicknames and there is no stock-exchange floor. The modern world has done its best to sanitise the City landscape. Trading is done electronically with a click of the mouse and market making is all but a sideline. Many fund managers even bypass the sell side altogether, entering their trades directly into the market via algorithmic computer programmes.

Any technophobic rants are, however, misguided. People have adapted, not disappeared. Just as brokers have learned to re-invent themselves so traders have moved with the times, embracing progress and the benefits it brings. Technological advances have transformed financial services from quasi-cottage industry into multi-trillion dollar beast, enriching individuals beyond their wildest dreams and creating jobs by the thousand. This has had a direct knock-on to wider society, with the City's rise nurturing anything from restaurants and bars to furniture manufacturers, budget airlines and electrical goods retailers.

How it Works Today

Trading is not a homogenous activity; it is, in fact, a generic term for a series of inter-related functions. In the equity world 'trading' can be split into two camps: a) executing client business ('execution') and b) investing your firm's own capital ('proprietary' or 'prop').

Boutique firms don't tend to risk their capital (unless they run small-scale market-making operations – more on this later), and are consequently known as 'agency brokers' (because they act as agent and nothing more). Investment banks, however, muddy the water by committing capital in both their execution and proprietary businesses. To make matters even more complicated, some firms run the two businesses side by side, while others segregate them. There are advantages (and disadvantages) of doing both, which we'll come to explore.

Execution: Stage 1

In its simplest form, execution works as follows. Fund manager Arvzees Capital wants to buy a million shares in BP. He can either a) contact a broking firm himself or b) get a dedicated colleague known as a 'dealer' to do it for him. In the larger institutions (and in many of their smaller brethren) fund managers no longer get involved with the actual buying and selling of stock (or 'dealing'). This allows them more time to carry out their daily duties (such as speculating, pontificating, haranguing companies, eating lunch, playing tennis, etc) and leaves less scope for mistakes to be made (red wine and dealing aren't the best of bedfellows).

If a) then he has two further options. Once he has decided through which firm he wants to trade, he will call up/send a Bloomberg message to either i) a broker or ii) a 'sales trader' who, as his name implies, is a hybrid salesman/trader. We'll have more on him and what he does in a moment.

If b) then the dealer will call up/send a message to either i) a sales trader or, occasionally, ii) a broker. As a rule fund managers speak to brokers and buy-side dealers to sales traders, but there are always exceptions. These days the City is a tangled web and people don't always keep to their stations – there are times when fund managers do business with sales traders and buy-side dealers liaise with brokers. This is a relationship game and it all depends on whom you know best.

THE DEALER DOES have a third option – he might enter the order into an algorithmic trading system (supplied to him by an investment bank) and let the computer take care of everything else, a process known as 'direct market access' (or 'DMA') and favoured by the more active buy-side firms. The creep of technology is relentless and in the world of trading especially so. Very liquid (easily tradable) instruments such as equities can be traded just as efficiently by computer as by human hand and the systems can handle billions of dollars' worth of trade on a daily basis. Algorithmic trading suits both fund managers and their investment-banking counterparts – it's quick, cheap and hassle-free. Fund managers pay lower commission and spend less time liaising with the sell side while the banks compensate for the lower commissions by the need to employ fewer people. Of course, innovation doesn't always suit everybody. The smaller broking firms don't supply the systems and so suffer as business migrates away from them in ever increasing droves, while old-school traders, who are less trusting of progress, dismiss the technology, claiming that a man can beat a machine any day of the week. In the example below we'll assume that the fund manager in question doesn't have recourse to algorithmic trading.

Execution: Stage 2

A telephone is now ringing in a broking firm.

'Del Boy, it's Brian [from Arvzees]. I want to buy a million BP.'

Whoever answers the phone, be it Brian's sales trading or broking contact (or a colleague), will then ask for instructions as to how to proceed (unless Brian volunteers these first himself). Typical dealing instructions concern price (the client may have a limit he doesn't wish to exceed), volume (if the order is a large one it makes no sense to flood the market and spike/collapse the price) and time (there may be an hour's limit, a day's limit or no limit – whatever the client wishes).

Fund managers and their dealers prefer to pass trades through sales traders rather than through brokers. The reason is simple – the latter spend their days at the coalface of the market, chewing the cud with colleagues, clients and competitors in an effort to see which way the wind is blowing (indeed, some sales traders are renowned for their expertise in certain sectors and even in certain stocks). In other words they're dealing professionals.

Most brokers, by contrast, can't make this claim. They have neither the contacts (most fund managers are similarly removed from short-term market fluctuations), nor the time (much of which they spend handing out coffee in meetings) nor the inclination (trading is still regarded by many as a blue-collar vocation) to provide a comprehensive trading service. As we shall see, sales traders spend all day at their desks (give or take the five-minute constitutional they enjoy with that morning's tabloid newspaper, staring transfixed at their screens and alerting each other to (often minuscule) market moves.)

'Fuck me, Bobby. Have you seen the way these oils are jumping? BP's just rallied half a per cent.'

'What's going on, Del?'

'Hang on, I'll ring George and see if he knows the score.'

*   *   *

'George? Del Boy. What's the form in these oils?'

'Not sure, mate, but there's a story doing the rounds about Saudi supply shortages.'

'Cheers, big ears. Ring me back if you get any more, will you?'

*   *   *

'Carl? Del Boy. You got any scoop on BP?'

'Hold on, mate. Yeah, we're hearing that Credit Suisse have upgraded the sector.'

$

AS A GENERAL RULE reading the newspaper (even the financial press) at your desk is a definite no-no. Most people, if they want to read the paper, smuggle it off to the lavatories inside a piece of research. Management know exactly what's going on but do nothing to stop it – they're all at it too! In *Bonfire of the Vanities*, Tom Wolfe's depiction of 1980s Wall Street hubris, Master of the Universe and hot-shot bond trader Sherman McCoy believed that, 'You headed straight for your desk, your telephone, and your computer terminal in the morning. The day didn't start with small talk and coffee and perusals of the *Wall Street Journal* and the financial pages of the *Times*, much less the *Racing Form*. You were expected to get on the telephone and start making money.'

Not so long ago the sales trader's rise was triggering predictions of the broker's demise, but this underestimated a) the latter's resilience and b) a fund manager's need for psychological support from a perceived social/intellectual equal. Although the roles have continued to elide to the extent that the industry is much more egalitarian than it ever was (indeed some traders are far more clued up and/or debonair than the average broker), perceptions take time to shift. Moreover, many traders seem happy to preserve the stereotypical divide, content to be cast as perma-tanned wide boys and/or lovable rogues. who provide the buy side with nothing more profound than a) dealing capability and b) short-term market intelligence, however misguided it proves. Most traders are like financial weather forecasters – everyone listens to them even though they're often wrong.

Indeed, there's no better barometer than a trader for ascertaining the level of market activity. As the cult of the hedge fund spread, investment banks saw new avenues for money making and 'prime broking' became an increasingly relevant and profitable City activity. A prime broker is essentially a hedge fund's surrogate mother and played an integral role in the industry's boom and subsequent bust (see *Fund Management* for an insight into how hedge funds work and why things went wrong). Prime brokers are divisions of investment banks that are, among other things, responsible for a) lending money, b) introducing capital providers and c) helping new hedge funds get established. If a bank could help a hedge fund get off the ground, so the theory ran, it would reap the rewards when the latter made it big.

For the sell side, prime-broking clients were a godsend. In return for leverage, capital and the key ingredients of a hedge-fund starter kit (tables, chairs, computers and an office in Mayfair), a hedge fund had a duty to pay a prime-broking parent the lion's share of its commission. As the hedge-fund industry mushroomed, traders struggled to keep up with demand. During 2003–07 it was Christmas every day. One trader entertained a client on a Thursday, overslept on the Friday and was woken at 10am by the telephone. The client's voice, thick and rasping, came down the line, 'If I can get to work on time you can too. Be there in an hour and I'll give you three months' worth of business. But if you're not then I'll never deal with you again.'

By the end of the decade, however, things looked very different. As investment banks turned off the lending tap, hedge funds disappeared down the drain in their thousands and the traders who were left sat sleeping at their desks, comparing dealing floors to morgues and honing golf swings in the corridors. But traders always love to moan that 'nothing's happening' or that 'this place is dead' and they, more than anyone, understand that the City is both seasonal and cyclical. What you don't do is abandon a friend who's fallen off his perch. There's a chance that one day he'll get up again and return the favour many times over.

§

HEDGE FUNDS ARE, however, free to chop and change prime broker. The Lehman debacle highlighted the extent to which banks and their prime-broking clients were entangled. We won't go into the complications, legal or otherwise, but when the vultures began to unravel the carcass it was discovered that Lehman had been lending so much money to hedge funds that in many cases it wasn't clear just who owned a hedge fund's assets. For a few extraordinary weeks in September and October 2008, hedge funds engaged new prime brokers and dropped others like hot potatoes. In a world where everyone and anyone could go bust, no one wanted to run the risk of having his assets locked up inside a bankrupt bank.

So when Brian calls Del Boy with the order, he expects to receive the best possible trading steer. Del Boy, on the other hand, has got to balance the requirements of the client with his own commercial obligations. If a trader knows on which side his bread is buttered (and most do), he'll let the former take care of the latter.

'Well, Brian, you see the stock's just spiked 2%? There's some rubbish about Saudi supply shortages, but I think it's more likely to be on the back of a CS [Credit Suisse] upgrade. If I were you, I'd stick on a 50 top [ie limit] and see what happens. I reckon they'll come back from here.'

In other words he's advised his client to set in place a limit, thereby running the risk that if the price doesn't fall, the trade won't happen and his firm won't get paid.

At this juncture Brian might agree or he might reply,

'No, Del, we'd better crack on. I want to get these done straightaway. Can you buy them in line with volume?'

Some clients don't leave instructions but slam down the phone as soon as they've given the order. If he's your client and you're accustomed to his ways then all well and good, but it can be a problem if you answer a colleague's phone and don't catch the caller's name. Problems can become nightmares when a colleague can't be contacted (eg he's away on holiday) and you're running round the office trying to guess a) who the client was, b) how to get hold of him and c) how likely he is to bite your head off for asking stupid questions! The issue is compounded if you can't understand what the client's saying. One of the most powerful Frankfurt fund managers used to bark orders down the phone in heavily accented English and then hang up, reducing already terrified traders to whimpering wrecks.

$

> BROKERS AND TRADERS are supposed to leave back-up plans in place for when they're away from the office, but many neglect to do so. They either forget or, as is more common, do so deliberately: in the City most people are paranoid. The last thing you want is to come back from holiday and find that a client and a colleague have been cosying up to each other, just as no man with any sense would go away on business and leave his young bride at the mercy of an avaricious neighbour!

Mistakes (or 'dealing errors') are a trader's worst nightmare and are more common than you might imagine (even when sober). Convicted fraudsters such as Nick Leeson might grab the headlines, but every day traders make innocent but careless mistakes that eat away at a bank's bottom line. You answer the phone, take down the order, enter it into the system and then. . . a cold, clammy panic sets in. Did you write it down correctly? Was it a buy or a sell? Have you inputted the right stock code (some stock codes can seem scarily similar)?

Sod's law dictates that dealing errors cost money. It's rare that you receive an order to buy a stock, realise too late that it's a sell and exit the position at a profit. More often than not the stock will have nose-dived, and you'll be scrabbling to cut your losses and start executing the client's order before he can scream at you for getting it wrong.

Most firms will cover your back if you make a mistake, especially if the loss is small or the error is honest. Others, however, are famous for their lack of charity and will do anything to pass the buck, from pinning the blame on the client to hanging the guilty party out to dry. One trader answered a colleague's phone and took an order to buy what he thought was Deutsche Telekom. It was only half an hour later, when he called the client to update him on his progress, that he discovered he'd actually been asked to buy Deutsche Post! As management stepped in to calm the client down, the trader held his head in his hands, staring down the barrel of a six-figure loss. Not long after, following a short but painful interview, he was packing his bags. He couldn't foot the bill and so he had to go.

Execution: Stage 3

The sales trader / broker will now enter the order and any instructions into an electronic system (which can be seen by all his colleagues), and will then:

a) Make sure everyone else has seen the trade.

Traders are relentless self-publicists. Telling the dealing floor you've bagged an elephant makes you look good, feel good and, just as importantly, gets under your colleagues' skin. Sales and trading are commercial operations where the individual is under constant pressure to justify his worth, and most people can't help but obsess over what everybody else is doing. On a typical dealing floor envy and *Schadenfreude* abound in equal measure. Don't be fooled if a colleague con- gratulates you with a smile and a slap on the back – in private he'll be gnashing his teeth and wishing the earth would swallow you up.

If someone comes up to you and says,

'That's a cracking order.'

What he really means is,

'How the hell did you get that, you lucky bastard? I wish that was mine!'

There's also a practical reason why you want colleagues to see the fruits of your labours. Broking firms are obsessed with what they call 'flow' (or 'natural') business. If a client is buying a stock then it makes sense to find 'the other side' (ie a client to sell it). That way the firm earns commission on both sides of the bargain and saves itself the hassle of going out into the market. Traders regard 'crossing stock' as an important weapon in their professional armouries.

As soon as Arvzees' purchase of a million BP appears on the screen, sales traders and brokers will be milling around Del Boy asking if they can help him cross the stock. All of them want to be able to call their own clients and say, swelling with self-importance,

'We've got a natural buyer of BP. Do you want to let any go?'

What happens next depends on Del Boy. Traders like to protect their clients' interests and their identities, and fund managers can be prickly about having their business bandied around (some even refuse to let brokers/sales traders share their orders with their colleagues). Now, buying a million shares of a stock as large and as liquid as BP (which will cost the client circa £4.5m plus any commission)[8] is not a life-changing trade, even if it's a good-sized order, but Del Boy may still choose to leave his colleagues out of the loop. What he doesn't want is for someone to whisper down the telephone,

'Arvzees are buying BP.'

And for this to get straight back to Brian and his friends.

8 Depending on the commission rate (most institutional investors pay anywhere between 0.05% and 0.3%), this will cost an extra £2,250 to £13,500.

As we touched on earlier (see *Equity Sales*), brokers and/or traders like to tell other people what's going on even if they shouldn't. Under FSA rules, informing a client what another institution is doing constitutes 'market abuse' (which means, if caught, the guilty party can expect a fine and the loss of his job). Some people seem to take no notice of this, suspected of discussing other people's business at every available opportunity.

AS WE SHALL explore (see *Fund Management*), not every investor minds his rivals knowing what he's up to. Some fund managers actively encourage indiscretion and employ the sell side as an unofficial public relations arm.

---

b) Decide how you want to execute the trade.

In the example above, Brian asked Del Boy to buy the BP 'in line with volume'. In essence, this is an instruction not to rock the boat. Whatever the number of shares traded in BP that day (ie the 'volume'), whether it is higher or lower than average, Del Boy must buy a fixed percentage so that he doesn't a) move the price when volumes are low or b) get left behind when the reverse is true.

If he doesn't want to cross the stock in-house then he has a couple of other options. He can either i) 'work' the order manually in the market or ii) promise all or part of the BP to Brian at an up-front, pre-agreed price, a process known as 'committing capital'.

Working an order in the market is the job of a specialised 'dealer' (not to be confused with the buy-side variety *à la* Brian). Being a dealer can be a gruelling existence. You can spend all day staring at banks of screens, juggling orders with the dexterity of a mathematical conjuror.

By way of example, Del Boy might shout across to Alan the dealer,

'Alan, can you buy me a million BP in line with vol? Cheers pal.'

Alan will be able to see the order on the system and, if he's not too busy already, will pick it up. Modern electronic trading systems are now so sophisticated that they can be programmed to do almost anything the dealer desires. In the case of Del Boy's BP, getting the system to buy one share in every ten that trade (or whatever the volume requirements are) until Brian has completed his order should be no trouble at all.[9]

Buying large, liquid stocks like BP is not difficult. Buyers and sellers of the shares are plentiful and price behaviour is never too volatile. The dealer plugs his requirements into the system and off he goes. As long as he knows what he's doing/stays alert, he should be able to beat the 'Volume Weighted Average Price' or 'VWAP', the Holy Grail for sales traders and dealers. VWAP is calculated from the time the broker/sales trader receives the order to the time at which he completes it.

If, on the other hand, a stock is prone to volatility and/or is illiquid, he might struggle. Blocks of shares can trade at rogue levels, thereby distorting the VWAP, and a dealer has only to blink and he's missed it. Saying he fell asleep (all too easy on a summer's afternoon), was smoking a cigarette or was watching the 2.20 from Ascot will cut no ice with Del Boy and co, who will now be dreading the

---

9 Unless he presses the wrong button, known in dealing parlance as a 'fat finger'. If you have an order to buy BP, get the decimal point in the wrong place and realise too late that the machine has gone ahead and traded, as you scramble to unwind the trade, dealers around the City will be screaming, 'BP – fat finger!'

inevitable lecture from the client. This is one reason why sales traders will look to cross blocks of illiquid stocks if they possibly can.

WHEN THINGS GET tricky human intelligence should come into its own. Executing a trade in an illiquid stock can often have a detrimental effect on the share price, and a dealer must do his utmost to be discreet. A client might want to buy a stock for which there is no obvious seller (and vice versa), and you'll need to pull out all the stops to track it down and coax it from its lair (by contacting existing shareholders/well-informed market contacts or tapping other liquidity sources such as alternative exchanges and 'dark pools').[10]

Committing capital or 'proprietary ("prop") trading' might be a way in which the big banks do favours for their clients, but from both the bank's and the client's perspective there's a perennial question mark against the value it adds (for a more in-depth discussion of prop trading and the wider challenges it now faces see *Fund Management*). Committing capital can detract from, as well as add to, the money a firm makes from commission, and trading against order flows can compromise the service a bank offers the buy side.

Banks use their capital to provide their clients with liquidity. As we'll demonstrate in a moment, rather than go out into the market to buy or sell a stock, a bank can help kick off a client's order. It can also back up analyst recommendations. Prop traders recognise that well-known analysts move

10 A 'dark pool' is an anonymous source of liquidity away from mainstream public exchanges. Institutional investors use dark pools to buy and sell large blocks of securities without showing their hand to others. Consequently they are less likely to trigger a sudden share price move – the investor's identity and the size of the trade are revealed only when the trade is completed.

markets (see *Equity Research*) and that money can be made by a) following their advice and b) offering liquidity to an investor to get him to follow suit. Stocks will often jump or fall in early trading as investment banks build positions and then unwind them as clients join the party.

In the case of our BP trade, Brian could phone Del Boy at any time of day (even before the market opens) and ask that he commit capital. For example, BP might have closed the previous day at 440p (ie £4.40) and Brian hears about the Credit Suisse upgrade at 7.10am. Because he suspects the stock will trade higher, he wants to buy part of the position now rather than take his chances when the market opens. Therefore, he gets straight on the phone and asks,

'Del, can you make me a price in "half a bar" [ie 500,000 shares] of BP?'

Del Boy will then confer with a prop trader (ie someone who trades the firm's capital) and see what he says. He too will have seen the Credit Suisse upgrade and will be working out how to balance the demands of Del Boy's client with those of his 'book'. He might reply,

'There's going to be some fun in these today. You can have a quarter [of a million] at 50 [450p] or a half at 5 [455p].'

In other words, the bank is prepared to sell Brian 250,000 shares at 450p or 500,000 at 455p. What's more, it might not yet have the shares in its possession but will have to go out into the market to find them.

Brian might then opt to buy 500,000 at 455p and ask Del Boy to purchase the balance in the market when it opens. If BP begins the day at 452p and he thinks the stock will rally further, the prop trader might choose to close out his exposure, balance his book and take a profit of three pence per share (which equates to £15,000). If he thinks the opposite, he might sit and wait. That is his prerogative.

Let's imagine he does nothing and waits until midday, by which time the stock has climbed to 460p. At this stage he decides to close out his position for a loss of five pence per share or £25,000. Whatever commission Del Boy has earned from the trade with Brian will be more than offset by the loss the prop trader incurs.[11]

This is a recurrent theme – banks suck in clients by providing them with liquidity and then squander a large slug of the commission they generate. Although prop traders have an advantage no one else has in that they can see client orders coming in and so have an insight into which way the mood is moving, they often get it very wrong. As the last few years have shown only too well, markets can swing in sudden, unexpected directions.

As a consequence prop trading is something of a poisoned chalice. As we'll explore in more detail later (see *Fund Management*), it's hugely lucrative when it works and horrific when it doesn't. For now the words of the poet Longfellow will suffice:

'And when she was good she was very, very good,
  But when she was bad she was horrid.'

PROP DESKS ARE paranoid about preserving their anonymity and concealing their positions from other banks. The last thing a prop trader wants is for everyone

---

11 If Brian pays 0.15% commission (which is a standard rate) and buys a million shares of BP at an average price of 457p, Del Boy will generate commission (before any charges payable to the London Stock Exchange) of £6,855.

to get wind that he's the owner of (or 'long') a stock that's falling or short one that's heading for the stars. Rival firms have a nasty habit of turning the screw – if you're short a stock and can't get out they're more than happy to ramp the price!

This is where 'inter-dealer brokers' (or 'IDBs') come into play. They sit between investment banks, help them unwind their positions and act as an extra pair of eyes and ears around the market. In the example above, where our prop trader is looking to close his exposure and buy back the BP, he might go to an IDB and ask him to find the stock. How the IDB does the trade is up to him. He can either work it in the market or cross it with a seller (such as an institution or another investment bank), thereby protecting the identity of the original buyer. The prop desk will then pay the IDB commission in the same way an investor remunerates a broker.

The smaller firms, on the other hand, can't afford to risk their capital – quite simply they don't have the resources to play the big boys' game. To commit capital you must be able to withstand a financial dagger to the heart, and most boutiques try to run a tight ship, raking it in when times are good and running for cover when storm clouds hover. Like so many notions, however, capital discipline is wonderful in theory but rarely, if ever, practised. Small firms (many of which are run by narcissists and/or egomaniacs) are just as likely as investment banks to splurge cash at the top of the cycle and hoard it at the bottom.

There is, however, a way in which the junior firms commit capital – market making. This is a relic from the stock-exchange floor. As we saw earlier, in an age before electronic trading, to buy or sell any stock you had to go through a 'jobber' and in the smaller, less liquid stocks this is still the case. It works in much the same way as it used to, except that market makers now sit on dealing floors alongside traders and brokers, and advertise their wares on a Bloomberg or Reuters screen.

If an investor wants to buy or sell a stock, a broker or sales trader will get a sell-side dealer to approach a market maker (who might belong to the same firm or to another – it depends on the stock). The market maker will then decide if he wants to play. His first priority is to his book, not the investor – there's no point him buying stock in a sinking ship if he knows he can't sell it or will have to offload it later for a loss. He also has many stocks to stay on top of (sometimes as many as 50 per person) and other rivals to compete with – for these reasons prices for market-made stocks are as much a function of a market maker's whims/how awake he is after lunch as they are an actual indication of what investors think a stock is worth.

THE LAST FEW years have been no less testing for market makers than they've been for investors. Despite the glut of inside information to which they are privy (small companies are notoriously leaky), market makers have had a torrid time, losing more money than they've made and causing some employers to doubt the wisdom of the enterprise. Junior stocks suffer disproportionately during market turbulence – they're more risky and as a result fewer investors want to own them.

---

c) Tie up any loose ends.

Once a stock has been traded you'll report back to the client. Most of the time the client will proffer his thanks, give you any booking instructions (an institution can have several accounts, in the same way that people have both current and savings accounts with their banks) and move on to another subject.[12] There will, however, be times when he queries the price.

'Brian? Del Boy. I've done those BP for you. You buy a million at 457.'

For a moment there's silence and then,

'457? But I make VWAP 456.8. That's miles out.'

How much fuss a client makes about what he considers a bad price depends on the individual. Some are zealous in their pursuit of brokers and traders, ranting and raving like children who don't get what they want for Christmas, while others are more laissez-faire, accepting that in trading, as in life, you sometimes have to take the rough with the smooth.

Ask any trader and he'll tell you the same thing. You don't press a button and get fantastic prices, even in today's electronic age, and some clients just need to realise that.

It's Not What You Know. . .

Traders get in even earlier than brokers (6.30am GMT is considered late in most firms), sit adjacent to brokers at desks piled high with banks of screens (like despots with CCTV obsessions) and are almost exclusively male. Females do exist but they must either a) have their wits about them or b) revel in/be inured to a climate of crudeness. There's a camaraderie/sharpness about trading desks that no other City department can emulate, and we shouldn't hide from the fact that women find much in male humour that is a) infantile, b) pointless and c) offensive. On the flipside, women who last the course can

---

12 We won't worry about how shares (and the money to pay for them) are passed back and forth between investors (a process known as 'settlement'). Suffice to say it is done swiftly and electronically!

be among the more popular members of the team. Traders can be both sexist and fraternal.

Before the market opens, traders run a similar gauntlet to brokers. Anyone who's late will be hauled over the coals (serenaded by klaxon, a round of applause or stony silence – it all depends on the firm/mood of the morning), and will be given the appropriate punishment. Most trading desks will then get together ahead of the morning meeting proper to discuss events such as moves in overseas markets or relevant issues from the previous day's trading.

Once this is over traders will get straight on the phone, passing on any relevant (in their eyes) observations to the client base. You shouldn't expect much in the way of in-depth company analysis, as many traders don't – indeed won't – read research reports and will focus no further out than the end of the day ahead (ask the average trader a simple question on company valuation and you'll receive a look of bemusement). Intellect is not a prerequisite but wits, intuition and persistence are. Much of the time you'll get an order because you called, not because of what you said. If you have to say something make sure it's something the client wants to hear. Different clients will want to hear different things.

'Brian? Del Boy. How are you, mate? Good result for your lot last night.'

'Well, it was only Wigan. Tell me, what's going on?'

'Got a mixed bag for you this morning. Upgrades for Thomas Cook, RWE and a whole load of shite Italian banks – don't say I didn't warn you – and downgrades for Metro, BT and Electrolux. We've had some good two-way in the food retailers and that looks set to continue. What else? Oh yeah – I'd say the insurers look vulnerable here. I'd be selling Swiss Re and Aviva.'

'Thanks mate. I've got some Novartis to buy. Can we start with 20,000 with a fifty-seven fifty top?'

*   *   *

'Carl? Del Boy. You all right, son?'

'Yeah, not bad, Del. How's life?'

'Couldn't be better, Carl, couldn't be better. The wife's getting me down but what can I say? I'm sending you something we've done on the Italian banks. We've upgraded the sector this morning and it all looks good. Ask the analyst if you want any details.'

'Thanks. Anything else?'

'We've had some form in the food retailers and I'd be selling the insurers – they look toppy here. We're also seeing buyers of Novartis.'

'That's cool. I might have something for you later. Keep me posted if you see anything in KPN.'

Some clients take an age to make up their minds (because of internal bureaucracy or a lack of courage in their convictions – see *Fund Management*) and thus come to a party too late, while others won't stand on ceremony and will be badgering traders, brokers and analysts well before the market opens.

'Del? Brian. What do you think the miners will do today? We're short Antofagasta [Chile's largest copper producer and listed in London] and the copper price has been rallying. Should we cut and run?'

'Mate, I'd stick tight if I were you. The market looks soggy to me.'

But fast forward two hours and,

'Del, I'm being killed in these miners. What shall I do?'

'Yeah, they're looking pretty perky, aren't they? I thought they would. Let's cut them.'

To the outsider there's something psychotic about the frequency with which traders change their minds and then forget they've done so. It's as if they all wallow in a permanent state of chronic amnesia.

For traders as for brokers, the most important maxim is 'know your client'. Work out what he wants to hear and you're away. Get him on side and he'll be your friend for life.

Indeed, many sales traders and buy-side dealers grew up together, went to school together and arrived in the City together, working as 'blue buttons' (ie runners) on the stock-exchange floor. As in many other walks of life, common ground and longevity form the tightest of bonds. They breed trust, and in the City trust breeds commercial gain. Is it so surprising that, despite broker and fund manager protests, traders reward their friends first, second and third? Blood is, after all, thicker than water.

This 'favour culture' might drive brokers and analysts to distraction, but in truth most struggle to do anything about it. A fund manager might ask his dealer to 'direct a trade' to a certain firm, but much of the time the dealer will have total discretion, charged with getting the trade done at the most advantageous price. If that happens to be via his best friend, who works for a firm that provides his employer with no other discernible service, then so be it.

SOME PEOPLE WILL do anything to keep a client on side. One sales trader was borrowing a client's apartment and returned there after a night of revelry. Discovering that he had no clean underwear and faced with the prospect of an alarm call one hour later, he washed his clothes in the sink and then searched in vain for a tumble dryer. In his disordered state, panic set in. What was he to do? Then he had a brainwave. He'd use the microwave. After all, it did the same job as a tumble dryer, only more quickly. So he set the timer to ten minutes and promptly fell asleep. A couple of hours later he woke to a charred and blackened ceiling. The microwave had exploded!

But traders have contacts in the most unexpected of places and are nothing if not resourceful. By the end of the day the apartment looked as good as new. With the boss's express permission (the client was one of the firm's most important), traders had downed tools, donned overalls and set to work with brushes, rollers and paint pots. To this day the client calls the trader 'Johnny Hot Pants' and doesn't know the reason why!

It's for this reason that many (especially traders!) regard trading/dealing as the most financially vital of all the sell-side services. Although fund managers will stipulate how much commission should be awarded to the individual broking firms, in reality buy-side dealers have carte blanche to overpay their friends. A broking firm without a recognised dealing franchise is like a car with two gears – it works but not very well – and as a consequence traders can have a quite disproportionate sense of self-worth.

This myopia can often lead to tension, with traders disregarding the long hours of relationship building a broker or analyst might put in with a client and the latter resenting the power the former wields in comparison to the perceived value they add. While its management would love to imagine a broking firm as separate parts of the same machine working towards a collective harmony, this is an all too quixotic vision. In the City, as a rule, everyone looks down on everyone else. Across the industry people might claim to be playing a team game, but you shouldn't be fooled – most, if not all, are out for themselves. One of the City's golden rules is that if something moves you grab it, and as a trader just because you pick up an order doesn't mean you can claim it for your own. As soon as you enter an order into the system, colleagues will be swarming around you asking who it's from and trying to establish whether or not they can pinch the credit. Even analysts aren't averse to approaching a trading desk and suggesting that an order is a direct result of their endeavours.

'Del, I see we're trading in BP for Arvzees. I had a great chat with the fund manager the other day.'

Cue a snort and the sardonic response,

'And I've been discussing the stock with the dealer for the past few weeks. Today's the day we decided to buy it.'

And as the analyst moves away, somewhat chastened, Del Boy will turn to Alan, Bobby and the rest of the team, shake his head and say,

'Just listen to these pricks! They think they rule the world!'

Traders play politics as well as anyone – they're a devious bunch. As for brokers (and any other member of the financial universe for that matter), pulling the right political levers matters as much as the revenue you generate. In this game if you don't shout you don't get recognised – there are so many colleagues swarming over the same client accounts that your contribution can be overlooked unless you stick your head above the parapet.

Traders earn similar pay packets to brokers. A top trader will earn well in excess of a million dollars, even in an average year, while someone lower down the ladder can still expect a healthy six-figure package.

Look around at the end of the day and there's always a trader emerging from the boss's office.

'Yes, Mr Maxwell, we had a brilliant day. The boys were on fire. We did a whole load of BP for Arvzees.'

'Well done, Del. Keep up the good work. Let's see if we can make it a record year.'

But some managers are nothing if not duplicitous. Later that day Mr Maxwell will cradle a glass of port and tell the Head of Sales (or some other pillar of the community),

'I had Del Boy in my office again this afternoon, slagging off the salesmen and telling me how wonderful he is. He's a sweet boy and great at his job, but he really is a fucking pain in the neck.'

Parlour Games

Traders don't leave their desks if they can help it. Nothing haunts them more than the thought of losing an order. A client wants to be able to pick up the phone and be certain that a friend is at the other end. If Brian calls up and asks,

'Where's Del Boy?'

He won't be thrilled if he's told,

'He wandered off somewhere 20 minutes ago and we can't find him.'

In this instance most clients will leave an order anyway, but if a trader's absence becomes a regular occurrence then they'll become less and less likely to bother. For this reason a trader's hours are more market-orientated than any other City protagonist. You arrive early, sit glued to your desk (even when nothing's happening) and leave at 4.31pm on the dot, rarely attending meetings during market hours and never staying late to 'catch up on research' like so many brokers and investors pretend to. A trader is like an air-traffic controller – if you miss something, however minuscule, all hell can break loose.

As a consequence, trading desks can constitute the most intense of City environments. All around you are people with whom you compete and from whom you can never escape. Some people don't make any secret of their antipathy, sitting opposite each other for years on end and never exchanging a word. A star trader summed it up when he said of his closest rival, echoing the stance of many others around the City: 'I haven't spoken to that arsehole in five years and I don't intend to start now.'

But others revel in the rough and tumble and become bosom buddies, covering for each other when things go wrong, standing up to the classroom bully (the boss and/or other traders) and lightening the mood when necessary. Whether stuffing fish into the boots of each other's Ferraris or cutting the sleeves off Jermyn Street jackets, traders and their passion for horseplay are the stuff of City legend.

Personalities differ too – not every trader is a lovable rogue or a laconic reminder of a bygone age. In fact there's a plethora of characters, a few of which we sketch out below:

a) Mr Snake in the Grass
Never short of a quip or a gag, beneath the toothy grin lies a steely resolve. Determined to get to the top of the tree by

any route possible, he works his socks off, glued to his desk for 12 hours a day. But be careful – he'll charm you by day and knife you by night, as much at home in the boss's office as in the local community centre.

b) Mr Misery Guts

Forever complaining that 'I'm so bored' or 'there's nothing going on', he spends all day submerged in gloom, moaning to anyone who'll listen about his ex-wife and her new husband's singular capacity for greed. The more he earns, the poorer he becomes.

c) Mr Good Old Days

Born before time began, he's been round the block more times than he cares to remember and has a store of stories that would put many a war hero to shame. A shoulder to cry on for both clients and colleagues, he's trapped between his wife and his doctor, always retiring and then changing his mind.

d) Mr What Might Have Been

Suntanned, cocksure and fading fast, life just seems to pass him by. Played professional football at sixteen, semi-pro at seventeen and for the pub team at nineteen, he had all of the promise but none of the luck. Now lives the suburban dream with his pit bull terrier, bottle-blond girlfriend and mock Tudor mansion.

e) Ice Man

Sleek, composed and seriously professional, his bite is worse than his bark. A charming exterior belies a monstrous vanity – in his life there's a strict hierarchy in which he comes first, second and third. His orders are never yours but yours are often his. Clients fear him, distrust him and always overpay him.

f) Mr Product Placement

Smooth, charming and debonair, this guy looks good, smells good and is going far. Image is everything – weekends find him decked head to toe in smart suits and designer labels, strolling through Notting Hill, checking in and out of Californian rehab clinics or cruising along the Cote d'Azur with expensively assembled women in expensively appointed cars.

g) Mr Marbella

Everybody's business is his business – he has an opinion on everything, from football tactics to EU border controls. Barrel-chested, good-natured and brimming with right-wing fervour, he'll wear plus fours at weekends (in slavish emulation of his bosses) and speaks in exaggerated cockney rhyming slang about other people's wives, plastic surgery and his villa on the Costa del Crime.

IF ANY GROUP can be trusted to stretch expense accounts to the limit it's the trading fraternity. Although these days they find it difficult to spread their wings at lunchtime, traders more than make up for it in the evenings, taking, like brokers, the view that rabble rousing is the surest way to a client's heart. Indeed, some tread a fine line between client entertainment and credit-card fraud. It tends to be more common in boom times (when compliance departments are more willing to turn a blind eye), but traders aren't afraid of paying the most munificent of bribes, expensing weekend breaks, foreign holidays and even furniture in an attempt to secure a client's favour (and his commission)!

Conclusion

A sociologist would have a field day with the modern City hierarchy. On the surface, at any rate, today's financial world looks nothing like the backwater of yesteryear, but dig beneath it and many of the old features remain.

Thirty years on and several technological revolutions later, traders are still living on their wits, scrapping for business, chatting up their friends and slotting into place above and below brokers and analysts. Old habits die hard.

Trading can be many things. It can be stressful (in that you never know what the market will throw at you from one day to the next), exhilarating (when you land a big order and the adrenaline flows), tedious (there can be periods of lull that last for weeks if not for months on end), raucous (as the banter cranks up), spiteful (as others stick the knife in), superficial (traders will say practically anything to get an order), technical (dealing in illiquid stocks requires no little skill) and political (you can't ever switch off in this job – if you do, someone will trample all over you).

Getting up early and guessing which way the wind is blowing is the preserve of those who man the market stalls of Spitalfields or Portobello Road. They, however, don't ply their trade for small fortunes. But City traders do.

Most traders know how lucky they are and so keep quiet – there's no point highlighting life's inadequacies if you're one of its beneficiaries. Is it really their fault there's so much money sloshing around the system? Of course it isn't – they didn't make the rules. Some other clever sod did.

EQUITY RESEARCH
OR ANALYSIS

*'Euphemisms are not, as many young people think,
useless verbiage for that which can and should be said
bluntly; they are like secret agents on a delicate mission,
they must airily pass by a stinking mess with barely so
much as a nod of the head.'*

— QUENTIN CRISP

DON'T BE UNDER any illusions – brokers and traders
don't have it all their own way in the race to claim the title
of City Bluffer Par Excellence. Much of the ammunition
with which they do battle is provided by the analyst
community, a less exotic but equally essential cog in the
City smoke screen. In many ways the analyst is the
investor's most duplicitous friend – objectivity is all too
often compromised by the meddling of other people or the
need to play politics. What an investor sees is not always
what he gets.

Analysts don't always believe what they write (and vice
versa). Badgered all day long by brokers, traders and
corporate financiers, if they want an easy life they do what
they're told. Analysts are purveyors of propaganda,
essayists in the pay of an evil regime – if they're required
to bend the truth, then bend it they will.

In a Nutshell

Research departments are the in-house libraries of broking firms and are where brokers, traders and investors go when they require information on a particular stock or sector. As an analyst you will research ('cover') a clutch of companies in a certain industry or sector. You must have an in-depth knowledge of how that industry works, be able to estimate a company's likely financial performance and have a view as to whether investors should buy or sell a given stock.

Hit the Snooze Button

Analysts arrive at the office at a similarly uncivilised hour to their counterparts in equity sales, but while brokers can get away with sleeping off the previous night's excesses at (or under) their desks, an analyst is afforded no such luxury. Most company announcements, scheduled or otherwise, comes across the news wires at 7am or just after in the form of an 'RNS[13]', and you have to be ready to interpret them in time for the morning meeting. This means you must arrive in good time, especially when you expect one of the companies you cover to be contributing something that day. It goes without saying that pleading illness/planning holidays on such occasions will not be well received.

In most firms the analysts will sit on a separate floor to their colleagues in sales and trading. If a dealing room is a hum regularly punctuated by whoops of exultation or machine-gun-fire expletives, an analyst department is a quite different experience, more akin to a cathedral or university library. Analysts do use the telephone – we'll come to this in a moment – but more often than

13 This stands for 'Regulatory News Service' and confirms that an announcement has been made via the official channels.

not will stare for hours on end at their computer screens in silent concentration.

Most mornings you'll be prepared for what's coming. We'll explore in due course the various ways in which you do this, but essentially companies and analysts join forces to make life easier for each other. On occasions, however, companies will be forced to reveal secrets they have been keeping from the market, thereby dropping time bombs on an unsuspecting City.

Many company announcements will be scheduled – companies like to make life easy for analysts and investors by giving prior warning as to when they will say something of importance. Companies report results two or four times a year, and more often than not reporting periods correspond to the calendar year (ie Quarter 1 or 'Q1' is typically January–March). For this reason results come in clusters and you will find that certain times of the year are especially hectic. Other scheduled announcements include trading statements and Annual General Meetings (AGMs) – both are ways of keeping the market up to date between results announcements. When a company reports its results you have to stand up and tell the brokers and traders how these results compare to your expectations.

What a company has or hasn't said one morning will be being scrutinised by a million other eyes – investors, brokers and traders will be all be watching, reading and expecting you to tell them what is going on. If one of the companies you cover says something unexpected, a trader or investor with $20m riding on the strength of your advice might call you and say,

'What the hell do these numbers mean? Revenues look OK but they've missed on the earnings. What's all this about a write-down in the US?'

Now you might have arrived at work at 6.49am, boiled the kettle at 6.53am and dug your spoon into your cereal at 6.59am. The numbers might then have been published at 7.01am, you started reading at 7.02am, spilled milk on your trousers at 7.03am and received the call at 7.05am. The statement is 20 paragraphs long and you're a slow but thorough reader. By the time the call comes in you're only on paragraph seven.

Much of the time the answers,

'I'm still having a look. Give me five minutes, won't you?'

Or

'Wait for the morning meeting',

will suffice, but in the City people aren't always known for their patience, especially if they're senior, well paid and endowed with a stratospheric self-regard.

'You've got five seconds, not five minutes. I've got a client on hold and he needs to know the answer NOW!'

Or

'You got me into this crap. Now find out what the fuck's going on.'

In the old days – that is, the really old days when you could smoke at your desk and morning meetings began after dawn (back in the 80s) – there wasn't the same need for instant gratification. Either everyone knew the answer already (confidential or 'inside information' could be passed from corporate financier to broker, trader or analyst without penalty – internal barriers, or the so-called Chinese Walls, didn't yet exist) or people were more patient. These days, however, analysts must learn the art of appeasement, keeping investors and traders sweet while encouraging finance directors to spill the beans.

In high finance, time + information = money. The sooner you have a piece of information the more quickly you can act on it. Most of the time information doesn't flow directly from originator to end-user but via a long and fractious chain, like a giant game of Chinese Whispers. What a chief executive says and what he means can be two quite separate things. Imagine how much more distorted things can become by the time his words reach an investor!

Drama School

If you have a taste for the theatrical then the morning meeting is your stage. For a young analyst forced to appear before his elders and betters this can be a daunting occasion, particularly in large firms when you must stand alone at a microphone and read from a script in front of row upon row of hatchet-faced brokers, your image beamed from and projected on to screens on dealing floors all over the globe. Even in the smaller, more collegiate firms where brokers, traders and analysts gather together in one room to hear that morning's pronouncements, the experience can be far from agreeable. Colleagues will do anything to discourage you from talking, from feigning disinterest, snapping pencils or sighing, to fixing you with the most hostile of stares.

At the start of your career you'll be assigned a sector and let loose on the stocks that don't matter. Sometimes your academic/industrial background will be a key determinant (eg a science degree might lead you into the chemical or pharmaceutical arenas), and if you don't have a specific expertise then you will be used to plug gaps in the department's portfolio. Sector teams are always on the look out for lackeys, and junior analysts are useful for performing the menial tasks everyone else would rather avoid (such as filling in spreadsheet upon spreadsheet of historical coal prices).

$

> DEPENDING ON THE sector you cover, analysts receive a range of different perks. While airline analysts have historically enjoyed the luxury of a gold card and hotel analysts have been whisked off to some of the world's most glamorous destinations, chemical or engineering analysts have been somewhat short-changed, forced to feign gratitude as they pocket yet another useless widget or test tube.
>
> But perks aren't always what they seem. One leisure analyst was invited to Manchester to take part in a football match between City representatives and Manchester United employees (of the non-playing variety). Intent on proving his prowess, he rose high at a corner, cleared the ball but rammed his head straight into the nose of the club's then finance director. He watched in horror as his client crumpled to the ground, blood spurting in every direction, his nose a broken and mangled mess.

Once you have been assigned to a team you will then work your way slowly but surely towards covering companies by yourself. At first there is much to learn in terms of both process and method, and you will spend hours observing, reading and entering numbers into spreadsheets. Forget all notions of intellectual rigour – writing research is all about process, and you'll soon get the hang of what is and isn't relevant. There's no point getting bogged down in something you think is fantastically clever if it makes no one any money.

When you are deemed ready (a state you will reach after

several months unless you are especially backward), you will be allowed to 'initiate' (publish research) on a company. This procedure is equally painstaking and will involve much background reading, several meetings with the company management and endless checking and double-checking by your elders and betters. Then, and only then, will you be allowed on to the microphone and into the lion's den.

---

§

SOME BOSSES ARE famous for training their analysts to the point of exhaustion, expecting them to dig deep into the minutiae of each and every company they cover. One individual would accompany his charges across the length and breadth of Europe, driving them to the point of murder as he chain-smoked cheap cigarettes and refused to let them sleep until they had sufficient mastery of their subject:

'One more time. What is the definition of working capital?'

'Inventory plus debits less credits.'

'Good. Talk me through Trigano's [small French company that sells camper vans] working capital management.'

Silence.

'I can't. . .'

'You should know this.'

'I know, I know.'

And as the analyst stalls for yet more time, all he's thinking is,

'Please can I just go to bed, you fascist? It's three o'clock
in the morning! What does any of this actually matter?'

Broking firms don't let inexperienced analysts anywhere
near blue-chip stocks (a 'blue chip' is a company of the
highest calibre, such as Rolls Royce or Coca Cola).
Important companies deserve important analysts, both
from the company's and the investor's perspective, and if
an analyst is going to get it wrong (which everyone does at
some point) then it's better he does it with a company
whose fortunes have no or little bearing on the firm's
revenues or its relationships with key investors.

Some brokers can be blunt to the point of rudeness when
a fresh-faced analyst steps up to the microphone (always
loud enough for the latter to hear). As you prepare to
make your debut, rehearsing the words in your head for
the umpteenth time that morning and suppressing the
butterflies in your stomach, you might hear somebody say,

'Look – it's another fucking graduate. Where do they get
these little bastards from?'

Or

'As if we care about that piece of shit stock. Fuck off back
to school, Harry Potter!'

As a junior analyst you must keep your public utterances
short and sweet. Stand up, get the message across and then
sit down. No one takes anything you say seriously and so
you must stick to the facts. After several years you might
acquire a reputation for intelligence/foresight, and then
and only then might you linger at the microphone and
pontificate. Even a senior analyst has a time limit – others
will wish to contribute and a sales force can concentrate

for only so long (just as their clients can concentrate for only so long at the other end of the telephone).

Indeed, it won't take you too long to shed your fear of the microphone. Once your face has been deemed to fit there's a good chance that, on any normal morning, half of the sales team won't have been listening to the slightest word you say. Many an analyst has returned to the sanctity of his department and asked the world at large,

'Do any of those dinosaurs give a toss about what I think?'

However, the sales team's apathy, real or imagined, doesn't give you licence to vanish from view. You might have any number of reasons for having to get up and speak. These include:

a) You cover a stock that has made an announcement that morning.

Let's now return to one of the morning meeting examples we encountered in Chapter 1 and explore what the analyst really meant. Here's what he said,

'This morning we have Q2 numbers from Martin and Wellbourne. Revenue was in line with expectations but EBIT was 5% short of consensus forecasts as discounting took its toll on the gross margin. EPS was 8% light thanks to the higher tax charge. Going forward the company expects the positive trend in like-for-like sales growth to be maintained. Early indications are that Q3 like-for-likes have been in the region of 2%. We maintain our full-year forecasts and our outperform recommendation, believing that on 7x EV/EBITDA the stock looks good value versus the peer group.'

And here's what he meant (but would never say):

'There've been some disappointing numbers from Martin and Wellbourne this morning. The company had to slash prices in order to reach its sales targets but kept all us analysts in the dark. This has been a disastrous recommendation – the more I talk up the stock the more the share price falls. I'm doing my best to deflect attention away from me and on to the rest of the team and would change my mind if only I had the balls, but we're trying to win the brokership [ie become the company's corporate broker] and Corporate Finance need me on their side. I'll stay positive, hang my hat on a couple of spurious arguments and pray that in six months things aren't as bad as they seem.'

Of course, there are numerous occasions when an analyst tells it exactly how it is, but on many others a broker or a trader will have to read between the lines. An analyst is either doing somebody else's bidding or protecting his own back, persisting with recommendations that have turned sour because he a) wants to be proved right or b) has fallen in love with a stock and can't/won't see the reality. We'll have more in due course on the love affairs that occur between analysts and the companies they cover.

b) You have published some new research.

Let's now take the second morning meeting example from Chapter 1. The analyst said,

'You'll find on your desks a report we published last night on Automobiles de France. We maintain our in-line recommendation. Despite our conviction that the sector has turned something of a corner, we feel this has been fully discounted by the market. Susan and I will be laying out our arguments in greater detail at midday today.'

And here's what he meant (but would never say):

'I'm under pressure to talk about Automobiles de France. I have nothing new to add on the stock or the sector – in fact I'm not sure which one I hate more – but if I don't say anything at least vaguely positive then the company will be upset. More to the point, I have my bonus to think of and need to write something, however inane, that keeps me at the forefront of colleagues and investors' minds. I've spent three weeks on this report and still haven't come to a conclusion. Feel free to let me bore you all the way through your lunch break – we can then go and repeat the trick with your clients. Thank God I have Susan, my junior, to do all the hard work for me.'

In the City it's hard to say nothing, even if you have nothing to say. It's honest, yes, but not prudent. An analyst who keeps his mouth shut soon becomes commercially redundant, and if you want to get paid then you need to be noticed, it's a simple as that. In the weird and wonderful world of the sell side, bad advice is better than no advice.

c) You have visited a company and are reporting your findings.

In the City people love exclusivity, and analysts are no different. They're forever boasting about the proximity they enjoy to key corporate contacts.

'I've just returned from the Apple investor day where we were granted an exclusive meeting with their Head of Design. I've seen the iPhone 7 prototype and can confirm that it really is as brilliant as they say.'

Drawing a distinction between what is 'exclusive' and what is 'inside' is a wonderfully grey area. In other chapters (see *Fund Management* and *Corporate Finance*) we have more on who lets things slip to whom and why, but most analysts neglect to mention/prefer to forget that there is rarely such a thing as publicly available, exclusive information, especially where a blue-chip company is concerned. If an analyst announces in public that he has 'exclusive information' which is in fact 'inside information' then he's an idiot, and if it's 'exclusive' but not 'inside' then more often than not he's either a liar or a fantasist. In these sanitised times most large companies are intent on playing the straightest of bats and what they tell to A they'll tell to B, C, D, E and so on.

Smaller companies, on the other hand, tend to be less paranoid, welcoming anyone who'll listen (or who can be bothered) into the circle of their closest confidants. Analysts who take the trouble to visit the more far-flung parts of Europe can often return with the most useful (and fruity) of insights.

d) You say something spurious in order to do the boss (and yourself) a favour.

This is a useful tactic on quiet mornings when nothing much is going on and the Head of Research – your big boss – is desperate to find contributors to that morning's meeting. Mondays and Fridays are both good bets for such an eventuality, especially outside company reporting periods (see the next section). Being a 'filler' or your boss's 'go-to' man in a time of trouble will do you and your prospects no harm at all. If you say,

'There was an article in the trade press this weekend talking about governmental pressure on large retailers to cut electricity usage. This bodes well for the likes of Siemens and their voltage-regulation products.'

You demonstrate a) your commitment to the job (by scouring the more abstruse sections of the press at the weekend) and b) your ability to weave ideas from the most threadbare of material (which brokers and traders will love you for). The fact that you fabricated the idea is irrelevant – in the City something that sounds plausible is plausible.

Playing James Bond

The good analyst walks a veritable political tightrope. The ultimate double agent, he has to balance two very different and often conflicting sets of requirements, those of companies and corporate financiers on the one hand and of brokers, traders and investors on the other. And, as we shall see, you need them all lined up on your side if you want to get paid what you think you're worth.

One of your duties as an analyst is to 'model' the companies you cover. A model is a spreadsheet where an analyst projects the financial results that he expects a business to make, and can constitute anything from a brief summary to a ten-sheet, 700-line blockbuster. Some analysts build models so complicated that it takes them most of the morning to turn on their computers!

Financial wisdom states that a company's equity value should equate to the present value of its future cash flows (or in plain English: what a company is worth to its shareholders should be equal to the sum, in today's money, of all future profits). If we hold that to be true, then an analyst's raison d'être lies in being able to establish that value. In theory a stock that is trading below its supposed value should be bought (and one that is trading above should be sold).

In the City, however, theory and reality bear little relation to each other. Things are rarely worth what everyone thinks they should be. Each and every asset class, whether it be shares, bonds, commodities or currencies, will often move in what appear to be counter-intuitive directions, pushed and pulled by a seemingly random force. Politicians, terrorists and natural disasters all vie to wreck the best laid of theories. Timing matters too – in volatile markets you can be very right on a month's view but very wrong on one or two weeks' view (and vice versa). In this industry so much depends on luck.

As a consequence, financial analysis is highly subjective. No opinion is wrong until proven otherwise. For this reason ten analysts can derive ten very different but equally legitimate estimates of a company's worth, depending on the assumptions each plugs into his model.

Numbers form the basis of financial analysis. For all the fine words that management teams employ to dress up their strategies or conceal their failings, investors will draw their conclusions from the numbers. If a company's results fall short of analyst projections then more often than not the shares will be punished (and vice versa).

Companies know this and set their stalls out accordingly. In other words, they employ analysts and their numbers to guide investors towards what they want them to think. Financial analysis is ultimately about the manipulation of expectations.

Companies influence analysts in three main ways:

a) Guidance

Without outside help financial modelling is more art than science. At the end of the day it's educated guesswork, akin to looking into a crystal ball and trying to predict the future. You can spend hours agonising over whether a company will grow its sales 5% or 6% and what knock-on effect this has on profits, or you can flip a coin and hope for the best – you've got just as much chance of being right.

But most analysts receive outside help – we know this because on an extraordinary number of occasions the world's largest companies report results 'in line with analyst expectations'. And human beings, never mind analysts, just aren't that prescient.

Companies give analysts help in that they tell them what to assume/estimate in their models. This help is known as 'guidance' and is an invaluable analytical short cut. When building a model most analysts phone the company finance director and/or investor relations manager and get him to build the model for them.[14] If they didn't then their different projections would be all over the place.

Such chicanery is perfectly legal and is mutually beneficial. The analysts get to put their feet up *and* look clever, while the company executives get to hobnob with City luminaries and talk their share price in the required direction. The provision of guidance leaves little room for nasty surprises. Sometimes management teams will cheat and be deliberately downbeat – when the company next reports its results it will then 'beat guidance' and give the requisite boost to its share price.

Large broking houses wield big sticks and their analysts move markets. The City watches closely for analyst 'upgrades' or 'downgrades', especially when the analyst in question works for a firm with the requisite clout. In most investment banks traders back up analyst recommendations with the firm's capital, thereby causing

14 Another shortcut is to find out what estimates your competitors have – such information is freely available – and to position yourself in the middle of the pack. There's no point looking stupid/sticking your neck out if you don't have to.

the stock to move in the intended direction and encouraging investors to follow suit (see *Trading*). As a young analyst you may be gratified to see your firm's or even your own name being attributed in the financial press to a share price's move the previous day. One junior was especially delighted when the *Sun* quoted him as its authority on the UK anti-smoking proposals and the effect these would have on the restaurant industry!

$

> ONE THING YOU'RE not allowed to do, whether you're a broker, analyst or trader, is 'front run' research. In essence, this means calling up a client and alerting him to the fact that a market-moving piece of research is about to be published. People do it all the time and very rarely get caught, but in theory it constitutes an regulatory offence, punishable by a fine or, in severe cases, disqualification from the industry.

But guidance can also mislead. There are times when the prospects for a company can turn swiftly and suddenly in an unexpected direction. A key customer might cancel an order, a factory might burn down or management might simply be lying. If things take a turn for the worse then a company is duty-bound to tell the market, and you as an analyst must keep on your toes. As you sit slumped amid a sea of screens and papers wondering how it could all have gone so wrong, brokers and traders will be demanding your head on a plate.

Things to watch out for include: profit upgrades (good), profit warnings (bad), takeover approaches (good or bad depending on the terms of the deal), acquisitions of another company (ditto) and management departures/arrivals (good or bad depending on the individuals concerned).

In general, the reliability of guidance depends on the predictability of an individual company's business model. It is harder, for example, to second-guess the future financial performance of a retailer or software company than it is of a builder or a specialist engineer. The longer-term nature of their business models means that builders and engineers tend to be able to predict in advance how much money they're likely to make at certain times of the year. By contrast, a retailer will suffer if a sudden spate of bad weather means that people stay at home and don't go out shopping.

If brokers and traders want to know whether a company's results are better than, worse than or in line with your expectations, investors play a slightly different game whereby they collate the projections that various analysts have for a given company, derive an average (or 'consensus') and then compare and contrast this with the actual result. As a consequence a share price might rise if a company's results fall short of your expectations but exceed those of consensus (and vice versa).

ANALYSTS OFTEN FAIL to acknowledge the outside help they receive, preferring instead to indulge in self-congratulation and narcissistic fancies. Ever loath to admit themselves at a loss, most will claim to be a dab hand at management, able to run the companies they cover so much better than the incompetent incumbents. After all, if anyone understands how a business works, it's them! As an analyst at a leading investment bank once complained, 'If it had been up to us the credit crunch would never have happened – we'd never have let it. Goes to show what happens when you leave a bunch of idiots in charge of the zoo.'

b) Dangling the corporate carrot

People don't like upsetting other people – that's a fact of life. Much in the same way, analysts don't like upsetting companies. Slapping a sell recommendation on a stock or deriding its virtues will soon land an analyst just where he doesn't want to be – in the wilderness.

We have already seen how it helps to be close to a company. Imagine how tough it can be when the opposite is true and you are at loggerheads. Management teams will be vehement in their condemnation of those whom they think don't 'get' them. They'll tell anyone who'll listen that the analyst and his employer aren't worth the time of day.[15] Only the brave stick out their necks and say what they really think. If an analyst doesn't rate a company it's most likely he'll take the easy way out – he'll damn it with faint praise and hope that investors are intelligent enough to read between the lines.

Analysts act as spin doctors for their firm's corporate clients. They're a key conduit of information between the company and the investment community. If the client needs to enlist shareholder support then the analyst might be asked to do his bit, either by writing a positive note or by telephoning/visiting the key investors and making the case (even if you don't agree). Learning to button your lip/fudge the numbers will become a daily preoccupation. It's one of the reasons analysts are kinder about companies than they should be.

Covering a stock with which your firm has a corporate relationship does confer other advantages. In the UK you will often receive a company's numbers the night before

15 This invites another question – what right does someone who has never worked in the 'real world' have to lecture experienced company executives on how to run their businesses? Many analysts join the City straight from university and have no relevant industry background.

everybody else and so are fully prepped by the time the market learns the truth the following morning. You will also have the ear of the management team in a way few of your competitors will have. For this reason investors will always want to talk to you – getting an edge in this industry is a constant preoccupation.

$

MANY OF THE larger quoted companies employ ex-analysts in their investor relations departments, some of whom enjoy extremely cosy relationships with the analytical fraternity. In an instance of 'I'll scratch your back if you scratch mine', there are analysts who receive no-holds-barred corporate access in return for writing favourable research. An attractive female investor relations executive once took this approach to an extreme, promising (and delivering) sexual favours in return for positive PR spin!

Corporate considerations act as a major restriction on what you can and can't say. If your organisation acts as corporate broker to the company or is hoping to win an investment banking role then the last thing your bosses will want is a research note from you highlighting the inadequacies of the business and its management team (see *Corporate Finance*). Over the last two decades investment banks have built up vast research capabilities with the sole intention of winning lucrative corporate mandates. Back in 1999–2000, 'TMT' (Telecom Media Technology) teams mushroomed in size as the sector exploded and banks and broking firms jostled for advisory roles and IPO and placing business. The greater their expertise/the deeper their resource, the more likely they were to be involved. Units that once supported two or three people suddenly housed 23 as firms sank capital into the space and waited for the deals to roll in, regarding equity research as a loss-leader for their more profitable operations.

The excesses and misdemeanours of those years gave rise to a regulatory backlash. As firms fell over themselves to advise on dubious mega-mergers and float companies they wouldn't wish on their fiercest foes, the authorities bit back, slating analysts for their lack of objectivity and demanding that Equity Research and Corporate Finance be fenced off from one another.

These days analysts are, in theory, not supposed to know what their colleagues in Corporate Finance are up to – New York State Attorney General Eliot Spitzer claimed to have eradicated once and for all the culture of connivance and to have made conflicts of interest a thing of the past.[16] Broking firms now go out of their way to issue disclaimers – in other words they warn investors when they have a corporate relationship with a company and assure them that there is no such conflict.

$

DISCLAIMERS ARE NOTHING if not environmentally unfriendly. These days a 'one-page note' is in fact an 'eight-page note' once one takes into account the reams of legal jargon that accompany each and every research piece.

But human nature doesn't change – it adapts – and money conquers all. An investor with his wits about him will still tread with care – only the naïve would believe that an analyst would be permitted to trash a stock at whose door his colleagues in corporate finance had been beating.

16 In 2003, in Spitzer's most famous case, star technology analyst Henry Blodget was charged with civil securities fraud after Spitzer published Merrill Lynch emails in which Blodget gave views on stocks that conflicted with what he had publicly stated. Although he neither admitted nor denied the allegations, he was banned from the securities industry for life and forced to pay a $2m fine and a $2m disgorgement (ie relinquish profits he had obtained by illegal or unethical acts).

Whatever the authorities do or say, some Chinese Walls will always be thinner than they should.

c) Pillow talk

Some management teams have silver tongues, adept at talking analysts into falling in love with them and their companies. Even when they're wrong the loyal analyst backs them to the hilt, convinced that their strategic vision is more pertinent than ever before, and issues that others claim to be grievous are in fact no more than minor irritants. He'll throw in the towel only when the stock is on its knees or when the management have been removed – his capitulation is often a signal that things can get no worse and that the share price will soon start to climb.

In light of all the above, the following statistic should come as no surprise: analysts publish far more 'buy' than 'sell' recommendations (on occasions the ratio has been skewed as much as 95 to 5 in favour of the buys, a stunningly inaccurate assessment of the realities of corporate prosperity). Like most people they're optimists, and in a world of limited accountability (people rarely go back and check how often you're wrong or right) it's easier to upset an investor than a company – one might forgive you but the other definitely won't.[17]

Croissants with the Competition

It's typical that on the day a company announces its results it holds a conference call or results presentation some time

---

17 Never mind buy or sell recommendations, some analysts are so indecisive that they spend whole careers sitting on the fence, penning nothing but 'long-term buy' (ie you should buy it at some stage but not today) or 'hold/neutral' (ie it's worth today exactly what the market says it is) research reports. Although some firms axe them for being non-commercial, others indulge them as if they're some harmless, long-standing member of the family.

later that same morning. This allows the analysts and investors who follow the stock to ask management questions about the company's performance. As a sector analyst you will encounter the same faces at the same meetings – these are your rivals from the different broking firms.

For a variety of reasons results presentations can be unedifying occasions. Just as brokers rush to curry favour with celebrity management teams, so analysts do the same, trusting that the brilliance of their observations will cause chief executives and finance directors to leap from their seats and punch the air with delight.

The analytical world is as hierarchical as any. In company presentations and on conference calls analysts from the big houses hold all the aces. First the chief executive and/or finance director will say a few words and will then take questions from the floor. Up will go a thicket of hands. For several seconds the CEO/FD will peruse the room, pretending to weigh up the claims of the various questioners, and will then invite the Goldman Sachs analyst to speak. It doesn't have to be Goldman – it could be any of the big boys. Just as long as it's someone who won't ask awkward questions and/or works for a firm everyone's heard of.

'Morning guys, Greg from Goldman here. May I first congratulate you on a superb set of results?'

'That's very kind, Greg. Thank you.'

'I've got three questions if I may. First, can you give us more detail on restructuring costs going forward and hence underlying EBIT margins? Second, in my model I assume you ramp up capex [capital investment] from Q2 of next year – is this still the plan? And third, you alluded to cost pressures in the statement. Could you give us more colour? Thanks.'

And, as Greg sits down, the CEO/FD will beam fondly, thank him for his questions and the charade will begin.

When Greg's questions have been addressed, John from Morgan Stanley will take the stage. John will be as well groomed as Greg, will ask similarly calculated questions and will bask in the same fond smiles from management.

And so it goes on until eventually the small fry emerge, blinking, into the sunlight. Now, analysts are not a homogenous bunch – many have their quirks and eccentricities. For every Greg or John with piercing eyes, an MBA and an Aston Martin in the garage, there's a Nigel with dishevelled hair, a battered briefcase and the demeanour of an antiques dealer.

'Morning, it's Nigel from Société Nulle Part here. Just a couple of questions if I may.'

This is the cue for everyone, including the management, to groan and look at their watches. If Nigel behaves true to form he'll ask a question so preposterous in its irrelevance that everyone else will snigger like schoolboys. They're laughing at him not with him – this is old-fashioned playground bullying. Analysts are no less spiteful than brokers when it comes to ganging up on the weak.

IF THE FACT that company results meetings are no more than staged charades needed any reinforcing, first thing that morning management will hold a series of private telephone conversations with the analysts who count and get any difficult questions out of the way. Don't be under any illusions – there's no such thing as a level playing field where financial analysis is concerned.

Talking a Big Game

Even if you're not the out-going type you won't be able to hide out in your research bunker. On a daily basis brokers, investors, traders and corporate financiers will badger you for information, views or reassurance on a whole variety of subjects, and if you want to get ahead then you'll have to co-operate with them all.

For analysts, as for brokers, the appearance of diligence is as persuasive as the reality, if not more so in the case of the former. While a broker is evaluated in part on the levels of commission he generates, an analyst's contribution is much less tangible. If you cover a small sector like leisure, for example, you'll never bring in the amount of business that a colleague who covers oil or pharmaceutical stocks can expect to.

More important than commission is the perceived contribution that you make to the firm. The general rule is that if you shout loudly you get noticed – this is no place for the meek – and if you get noticed you'll occupy a higher rung on the departmental ladder.

In other words, getting well paid is all about self-promotion. Let's now look at some of the people who can help propel you forwards (and drag you backwards):

a) Brokers

We have already commented on how brokers need analysts. Without an analyst by his side most brokers would founder. Analysts provide ideas, validation and, most importantly, credibility. They understand accounting, valuation methodology and industry trends. An analyst is a broker's commercial alibi – to most investors an idea without an analyst's stamp is like a leg of lamb without food standards approval.

But analysts need brokers too. Brokers talk to traders (and tell them which analysts they think are any good) and brokers talk to clients (and do the same). They provide the means by which analysts meet investors and get to air their opinions, and without an audience for their ideas analysts are all but redundant. Ultimately, as we'll come on to soon, how the buy side views the analyst community contributes in no small way to how much you earn.

As a consequence the need to get on with/cosy up to brokers is paramount. Brokers favour analysts whom they believe a) talk sense, b) are relevant and c) have the necessary clout with investors. It doesn't take long to convince brokers of an analyst's fallibility, and if you bang on about stocks no one cares about (because they are too small or obscure) then no one will listen, even if you're right. The more credible/relevant you are, the more clients you'll meet – it's as simple as that.

But brokers can also drive you to distraction. In most cases your intellectual inferiors (or so some colleagues would have you believe), they treat you like the steward in their local club, seeking your opinion and then never heeding it. Be careful if they ask to see the management of one of your stocks. You can't refuse – it would be like a teacher neglecting a call for help from a simple but earnest child – but more often than not they'll forget the request as soon as they've made it, meaning that the hours you've spent chasing the company, polishing your model and drafting sensible questions will have all been in vain. Analysts hate nothing more than trying to round up brokers for a company meeting only to be told,

'I'm on the phone. Yes – it's a client. I'll be there in a minute.' (And then they never show up.)

Or

'I'm sorry but I can't make it. It's my daughter's half term and we're going to the theatre.'

Or even

'Oh – didn't I tell you? I've got to collect some dry cleaning.'

b) Traders

We have already touched upon the fact that analysts and traders can have strained relationships. Each looks down on the other for different (and often erroneous) reasons – analysts on traders for a lack of academic nous and traders on analysts for being socially gauche.

If they can engineer it, each would rather approach the other via an intermediary – the broker – with both venturing rarely and with trepidation into the other's territory. Many analysts regard a visit to the trading floor as a virgin might a crack den, while most traders feel as comfortable in a research department as they would in a monastery. Traders don't read research reports if they can at all avoid it.

Put bluntly, the two don't understand each other – they very rarely speak the same language. If an analyst is trying to give a trader a long and reasoned insight into why something might or might not happen, the latter might interject,

'Look, cut the crap. Just tell me – is this piece of shit going up or down?'

But, like it or not, there are occasions when they depend on each other. In the same way as brokers, traders rely on analysts to help find ideas, navigate the mysteries of the market and decipher the implications of company announcements, while analysts need traders to help back up their recommendations, either with a client's capital or their own. It's for this reason that analysts report their findings to traders before they report them to anyone else – they'll do anything to avoid the latter's sharp tongue!

PROPRIETARY (OR 'PROP') traders – ie those who invest their bank's capital – often use analysts for more nefarious reasons. Having an analyst who can move markets is a powerful piece of artillery, especially if the trader has a position he wants to exit in a hurry. Alarm bells can ring when banks put out buy or sell recommendations: pushing the merits of a certain stock may be a sign that a firm has a long position it wants to unwind (and vice versa). In some firms analysts exist only to serve the prop book and its thirst for ideas (see *Fund Management*).

c) Corporate Financiers

We have already mentioned that analysts have an obligation to the firm's corporate clients, Chinese Walls or no Chinese Walls, and investment bankers are forever meddling in an analyst's affairs. In many ways the two are close cousins – both devote their time to picking apart a company's report and accounts, modelling financial projections and sweet-talking company executives into giving them the answers.

The two come into contact most often when a broking firm is acting i) as a company's corporate broker or ii) as a 'placing agent'. The latter help place stock in both primary (such as an IPO or a capital raising) and secondary transactions (such as when a shareholder needs help placing a stake or when the firm has bought the stake with its own capital and wants to 'job' it on at a profit).

$

THIS IS KNOWN as a 'bought deal'. Rather than act purely as an agent and help a shareholder place a stake in the market (in return for commission), a bank will take the risk upon its shoulders, purchase the shareholder's stake with its own money and then seek to place this stake in the market at a premium to the price it paid (this way it gets to book a profit and the commission, much in the same way that prop traders operate). That, at least, is the theory. It's not unknown, however, for banks to misread markets and be stuck with stock they cannot shift.

In each and every case, the analyst has a duty to help promote the corporate client and hence his firm, even if his instincts tell him otherwise. Before they take on business, notably primary, corporate financiers will consult a variety of analysts, brokers and traders to see whether or not the deal can be done. It's on these occasions that some of the greatest conflicts occur. Corporate financiers want to bag a fee and so pull one way while the others, ie the people who have to sell the deal, pull the other. Even if the deal gets sanctioned there are always other issues, such as whether the terms are right or the price is fair. Ultimately those who handle companies and those who talk to investors are two very different beasts – rare is the man who can empathise with both.

As an analyst your role in the primary process is as vital as that of a broker. If he has to go out and persuade his investor base to participate in the fundraising, you have to write the research and help convince the client that investing is the right thing to do.

Primary business can be time-consuming and gruelling, but its lucrative nature means that you must down tools and forget about everything else you might have been doing. Not only must your research be detailed and all-encompassing – in an IPO the company is making its market debut and you must therefore cover every angle – but the syndicate structure also means that you'll be at pains to outshine the competition. On such occasions your social life will wither and you will work late into the night, spending hours on the telephone with the company's management and driven to distraction by the corporate financiers forever hovering at your elbow.

Once the process has begun you will first present your views to the sales team and then to the investor base for what is known as 'pre-marketing'. This can take several weeks and, on large deals, can mean flying all over the world and acquainting yourself with hotel foyers and airport terminals. By way of example, you might fly to Denver from Paris for an hour's meeting and then on to San Francisco for another (where the client fails to show up) and finally on to New York (all in the space of two days). Pre-marketing road shows are generally dispiriting affairs. You'll spend weeks on a research report that investors are too idle and/or too cynical to read, and you'll then hold their hands and run through the reasons for buying a stock in which they have not the slightest interest. Some investors will refuse to see you, preferring to take their cue from the company management (whom the sales team will escort round afterwards in an attempt to clinch the deal).

In truth, the process can be an insult to your integrity. Obliged to argue the case for companies about which you might have major misgivings (this can be for any number of reasons – you might hate the business or simply think it's overpriced), you must play a straight bat and present an even straighter face to the investor. But fund managers aren't stupid – they know when something smells – and when they ask no questions, stand up 20 minutes before the meeting's appointed end and say,

'That was extremely interesting. Thank you very much',

you and the broker will know that the game is up.[18]

d) Analysts

Analysts may have a reputation for silent endeavour, but the chemistry (or lack of it) in your sector team matters hugely. Even in the larger firms, where research departments can comprise armies of people, many of whom don't know each other's names, how individuals communicate and divide up the workload is the key to success.

Analysts who are talented/in the right place at the right time can achieve celebrity status, and if you happen to be working for/alongside one of them then you should be carried along by the tide. Star banking analyst Meredith Whitney, once of Oppenheimer & Co and now running her own show, is a good example of this. Sectors move in and out of favour with the changing of the seasons – if your sector is hot and your boss is regarded as a guru then you will bask in the reflected sunlight, but be aware that markets are capricious and that darkness can quickly descend. Industries that were once popular can spend years in the wilderness – only now is the technology sector back in vogue after more than a decade in the darkness.

It's easy to tell when a sector is in vogue because the analyst will always be the first to speak at the morning

---

18 Something that really irritates fund managers is when a broking firm floats a stock, bags the fees and then forgets all about it, neglecting to write follow-up research and keeping the investors who bought it in the dark. Nothing is more likely to ensure that investors don't subscribe to your firm's next IPO!

meeting. When he falls out of favour – as invariably happens – he will be shunted towards the back of the queue. TMT analysts, once the stars of the show, soon became the forgotten men of research.

If your sector is in favour then don't quibble – thank your good fortune. We'll have a look at how and why bubbles develop in the next chapter (see *Fund Management*), but if you can (and many can't), try to go along for the ride and maintain your integrity. TMT analysts who said back in 2000 (and they did say it),

'anotherinternetfailure.com is cheap on 10x sales[19]',

were doing one but not the other, while those that said,

'anotherinternetfailure.com is crazily expensive on 10x sales, but the rest of the sector's on 14x so you might as well buy it',

were hedging their bets (correctly as it transpired) so that they didn't look stupid when the music stopped.

If an analyst is cunning he'll delegate all the hard graft (eg the construction of the spreadsheets and the writing of the research) to a junior colleague. He can then concentrate on what he likes best – putting his feet up on the desk, running his hands through his hair and telling other people what he thinks about the world. You'll soon notice how few of the so-called stars do any of their own work.

Having a star for a boss is a luxury, particularly one who lets you spread your wings or is prepared publicly to acknowledge your contribution. It's just as likely you'll

---

19 Calculating a company's value as a multiple of its turnover (or 'sales') is one way of assessing its value.

work for someone who impedes your progress by a) claiming the credit for your efforts, b) sticking a knife in your back or c) lumbering along in the slow lane – and that's no fun. Instead of calling a client and being able to say,

'Hi there, it's Joe Bloggs. I work for Pieter van Marle. Do you have five minutes?'

'Yes, I'd be delighted. I have as long as you need. Pieter is a great friend of mine',

you say,

'Hi there, it's Joe Bloggs. I work for Barry Smith at Bank of Irrelevance. Could I spend a couple of minutes running you through our thoughts on the retailers?'

'I'm sorry, but this isn't a good time. Where did you say you were calling from?'

Some analysts won't stand on ceremony – if they feel they're being impeded or undermined they'll do something about it, going over and above their boss's head and making their case. Those who sit there and take it, by contrast, will continue to sit there. It's like being back at school – suffering in silence doesn't make the bully go away or the matron come riding to your rescue.

e) Fund Managers

As you grow in stature and experience you will start to bypass brokers and acquire your own clients. These can either be your counterparts in fund-management houses (to whom account managers – see *Equity Sales* – will want to talk) or contacts you pick up during the course of time spent with brokers. Most brokers, if they rate you, will encourage you to speak directly to their clients – it strengthens the investor's bond with the firm, thereby obliging him to increase the commission he pays, and allows the broker more time to indulge in what he likes best – frivolity. Fund managers welcome it too – close contact with a clever analyst is a valuable asset.

Much of your time will be spent talking on the telephone or sitting down in a fund manager's office and exchanging opinions. This can be at your behest (for example when you have published a new piece of research), at his or at a broker's.

Meeting an investor can be daunting, invigorating or uninspiring – it all depends on the individual and the mood he's in. If he's a celebrated name or has a reputation for eating brokers/analysts for breakfast, then you must ensure you know your stuff and be prepared to stand your ground. Investors will have preconceived ideas of their own that don't necessarily tally with yours, and sometimes will attack you even when they agree with you out of boredom or irritation. There'll be other times when a broker has coerced his client into taking a meeting. Don't expect much enthusiasm on these occasions – even when they're awake some investors display all the animation of garden gnomes.

INVESTORS CAN HELP you as much as you help them. If they have a good idea it can suit their purposes to have you publicise it for them. Many of the sharpest (and most biased) analytical insights come straight from the buy side.

Sometimes an investor will ask you to come and see him on a certain subject, and when you put forward an opinion will interrupt you with,

'I don't think that's quite right. Have you considered the following?'

and will reel off a series of startlingly well-informed arguments. What you won't know is that as you entered his office building and went up in one lift, an analyst from a rival firm was coming down in another, and that the client is doing nothing more than regurgitate your rival's insights, playing a game of compare and contrast.

On other occasions an investor will call you and say,

'I've got Nike coming in to see me in half an hour. Could you send me over a list of questions?'

And as you slave away for the next 20 minutes or so, you'll wonder why on earth you're doing his job for him free of charge. A lawyer or doctor would never be so generous. And yet, as brokers and traders are also aware, this is the great paradox of the sell side, a world where you can earn a fortune for doing nothing and be paid nothing for doing everything.

Writing research reports on the companies you cover will be expected of you from time to time. These reports will focus on individual stocks or on the wider sector, and will include a valuation analysis (what you think the stock is worth) and a recommendation (whether an investor should buy, sell or hold the shares). They don't have to be thorough as long as they're regular, colourful and/or thought provoking – getting your voice heard is as important as being right.

In this industry public speaking and political posturing go hand in hand. Some analysts love the sound of their own voices and take every opportunity to grab centre stage, whether this is on the microphone, on the radio or in the business sections of the national newspapers.

In the City fresh ideas are in short supply. Most ideas are a) rehashed versions of old arguments and b) copied from other people. Most of the time people play it safe, but if you want to get noticed and can't conjure up anything brilliantly original then you might have to say something outlandish. If you write,

'In this report we challenge the consensus view that gold prices will remain above $1000 an ounce. We see a scenario where spot prices will fall back to $700 and below, and see downside for the following stocks of 50% or more',

people will sit up and take note. Even if they disagree, at least they're talking about you. As the old adage goes, there's no such thing as bad publicity. Now you might not even believe what you're writing, but the brilliance of the industry is this: you can justify anything analytically as long as it suits your argument. Remember – you're never wrong until proven otherwise.

> BE WARNED – THE desks of brokers and fund managers are always piled high with unread research reports.

It's no accident that analysts suddenly ramp up their research output and hassle brokers to take them round to see fund managers in the run-up to an account review or a survey vote. It's all about getting in front of the investor, even if you have nothing new to tell him. If you call him and say,

'The miners have performed very nicely since I wrote that

piece on them last month. Would you mind putting in a good word for me in our broker review/voting for me in the Extel survey?'

he's more likely to give his consent than if you say,

'The miners have performed very nicely since I wrote that piece on them last month. Would you mind paying me more commission?'

$

> SOME ANALYSTS ARE brilliant at begging for votes while others get very embarrassed about it. Much of the time it does no harm to ask, especially where surveys are concerned, as most fund managers won't remember to vote unless you remind them. And it's not like they're going out of their way to help you – they're only filling in a form. Corner one when he's weak – eg at an expensive dinner you're paying for – and thrust the form in front of him. Votes investors can hand round like confetti, commission they can't.
>
> Some firms encourage their staff to grab votes from wherever they can. It's not unknown for analysts to call up friends with whom they have no business relationship, or even fund managers whom they've never met and with whom they've rarely spoken. When it comes to votes, analysts are like politicians – they'll knock on any old door, no matter who's behind them!

As every firm cares about client account reviews, earning a fund manager's praise is essential, but where surveys are concerned firms are more ambivalent. As we have already mentioned (see *Equity Sales*), some care passionately while others couldn't care less. The latter either don't need them – their credentials are already established – or have better things, such as making money, to worry about.

It is true, however, that a top-rated analyst is a great calling card when a firm is looking to win corporate business, and as such a good survey rating can make a serious difference to your pay package. Needless to say, it's easier to get one if you work for one of the big boys.

Cattle Trading

The City is the ultimate cattle market – if you're half decent and the economy is on song then you'll get used to having headhunters on your case. Phones around the world may have stopped ringing post the Lehman Brothers collapse, but it didn't take long for the recruitment community to re-emerge. Like investment banks and broking firms, much of their work is deal-driven and the City is their lifeblood.

In actual fact headhunters are not too dissimilar to brokers. They call you up on spec, flatter your ego, pretend to be well informed and then make a tawdry proposition sound like the opportunity of a lifetime. Good headhunters are like good brokers – they're in the minority – but even the bad ones can come in handy.

Headhunters can be used to judicious effect by all City practitioners, even if it's not to move jobs. They can provide you with market intelligence (ie tell you what's going on at other firms) and/or help you get a pay rise. If you feel you're being short-changed you can feign interest in moving to a rival, go so far as to extract an offer and then use this as a bargaining chip with your employer.

This tactic goes only so far. Employers expect it from their staff, and most will play the game, match the rival offer if they consider you're worth keeping and call your bluff if you're not. But they tend to have their revenge when bonus time comes around – you're never held in quite the same regard once you've pulled the pay-me-more-or-I-move card.

> AGITATING FOR PAY rises can sometimes work against you. One analyst operated on the basis that a 'squeaky cog must get oiled' and would spend all day badgering his superiors, reminding them of his importance to clients and companies alike. Management eventually grew tired of his complaints and sacked him, reasoning that this particular cog was more superfluous than it realised.

People move around the City with abandon, changing jobs and firms with a frequency that makes professional footballers seem loyal. It's a skill in itself, but many make a sensational living jumping from firm to firm, collecting six– or seven– figure guarantees and moving on to the next before anyone works out that they're not actually very good at their jobs. This creates opportunities for other people, some of whom stalk the City like zombies, feasting off other people's scraps (in good times even the most mediocre people always seem to find employment). If the merry-go-round nets fees for headhunters, it creates headaches for investment banks – once they plug one leak another appears, thereby justifying the need for human-resources machinery of colossal proportions.

> THE ACT OF resigning seems to be beyond many people. Investment banks are past masters at getting you to reconsider what you imagined was a foregone conclusion, preying on your fears and tying you up in knots with threats, counter offers and persuasive rhetoric. If they don't want you to leave they'll wheel out the big guns, offering you once-in-a-lifetime dinners with head of this or the chief of

that and deluding you with a sense of your own importance. But once you've gone the people you've left behind will queue up to knock you down. Members of management will sit dolefully in wine bars and tell their employees,

'I told him not to go. I think he's made the most terrible mistake.'

Or (with greater vitriol),

'Good fucking riddance. He was no bloody good anyway. It's made not the slightest difference to our business.'

In recent years many analysts crossed the divide over into fund management and private equity, seduced by the newfound riches and offers of employment from clients who assured them they couldn't fail.[20] But as we allude to elsewhere (see *Fund Management*), many former analysts tripped up on their own egos, finding the transition to be far harder than they had imagined. Although the buy-side chaos and ensuing drought of jobs saw many analysts, brokers and traders scurry back to the sell side pleading poverty and begging forgiveness, traffic will eventually flow back in the other direction and research departments will once again be plundered for stars and opportunists. As an analyst your training, experience and contacts stand you in excellent stead for a variety of roles, from working on the buy side or in corporate finance, to joining a company whose virtues (and vices) you've had the pleasure of analysing.

---

20 Most firms don't mind letting employees go to clients if they think you'll direct business their way. In practice, however, it doesn't always work like that. Some people take great pleasure in sticking up two fingers and not directing a penny of business towards their former employer.

Working Hours

Unlike brokers and traders who get in early and slope off in time for the early evening news, analysts get in early and arrive home in time for dinner. There is a constant need to be seen to be doing something, whether this is updating your financial models, catching up with investors and corporate financiers, speaking to companies or putting the finishing touches to a research report (it doesn't matter if you're doing none of these things – it's the fact you're there that counts). In this industry face time matters, especially when you're young or unproven. Do you dare be the first to leave?

In most firms you'll escape anywhere between 6pm and 8pm, although there will be times (such as when you have an IPO research deadline) when you dine at your desk. The same is true if you have meetings to prepare for the following day. Don't be surprised if you find your workload impinging on your weekend – others will be putting in a few extra hours at home and you'll have (to pretend) to as well if you want to keep up.

Cashing In

How your salary is structured is the same as for a broker (see *Equity Sales*) – you receive a combination of basic salary and discretionary bonus (in the form of cash and shares). Even more so than in the cases of brokers and traders, don't expect your bonus to correspond to the revenue you have contributed to the departmental whole. As with his counterparts in sales and trading, your boss will be allocated a pool he must divide up among the troops, and you'll get better paid than most if a) your face fits, b) he likes you and c) you have pulled the political levers alluded to throughout this chapter. If you have colleagues, clients and survey votes all on your side then you should have nothing to complain about.

Top analysts are as well paid as their broking or trading counterparts, but the further down the food chain you sit the more you may find yourself casting envious eyes at the pay slips of your peers in sales and trading. Analysts some three or four years into the job can expect to be paid anywhere between 120,000 and 400,000, with those at the higher end working for the larger firms during times of plenty.

Conclusion

You need to have a brain to be an analyst, that's for certain, but it's not all about numbers, spreadsheets and long, lonely evenings. If brokers and traders shout loudly and get paid handsomely, analysts are aboard a similar gravy train, albeit one with a quieter engine.

Analysts don't spend all day locked up in gilded cages – some do but many don't. Like brokers and traders you have to sell your wares if you want to get noticed, and this means putting yourself in the shop window and flattering the egos that matter.

Equity research is turbo-charged accountancy. It's exacting without being exhausting and painstaking without being suffocating. It's the scholarship form at school with better pay and longer trousers. And, last but not least, it can be a springboard to bigger and brighter things – if you decide to pack it in you'll always have another home to go to.

In the superficial world of the sell side you're something of a rarity – you're a specialist – but don't forget to wear your heart under your sleeve. Much of the time you'll be suppressing what you think and saying what you disbelieve.

— 4 —

FUND MANAGEMENT

'It is not wise for a blind man, riding a blind horse,
to approach the edge of a deep pond.'

– Traditional Chinese proverb

IN THE CITY no one ever learns. Each and every generation is as greedy and as gullible as its predecessor. People make the same mistakes and buy into the same fantasies time and time again. For every bluffing broker there's a fund manager who thinks he's God.

The hedge-fund boom of the last few years is already coming to be regarded as one of the City's greatest fantasies. Long derided as staid, dull and (by City standards) badly paid, by the mid-2000s fund management had become the preserve of every bright young thing in town. Out went the slow but steady pension-fund manager in hotspots such as Brussels and Barnsley, and in came the trilingual aesthete with an office in Mayfair and a boat in Cannes. The revolutionary fee structure and the anything-goes investment approach (the more exotic the better) ensured that hedge-fund managers (and their pay packets) soon achieved legendary status.

But in 2008 the party came to an end – very few investors anticipated the cataclysm that was the credit crunch. One of its consequences was to bankrupt the premise to which the industry owed its explosion: that, regardless of market direction, hedge funds always made money.

In a Nutshell

A fund (or asset/portfolio) manager (or 'investor') is an investment professional who invests other people's money. How you invest and what you invest in depends on whose money you are managing and what level of risk that capital provider is prepared to accept. It generally follows that the more risk averse the capital provider the tighter the investment parameters within which you operate.

Via our savings most of us are exposed to fund managers. Pension funds, insurance companies, banks, charities, universities, government bodies and individuals the world over all control pools of capital that need to be managed and invested by professionals.

> YOU'LL REGULARLY COME across the terms 'institutional' and 'retail' to describe different providers of capital. 'Retail' essentially describes private individuals and 'institutional' the pension funds, charities, universities, etc, ie the corporate providers of capital.

A Mug's Game?

Spin doctors in the form of stock-market gurus and human-resources mandarins could be trusted to trot out the cliché:

'Equities, whatever the short-term fluctuations, always outperform in the long term.'

And the silver-haired denizens of the City would nod, encouraging their fresh-faced brethren to take note.

But proponents of the cliché have gone quiet in recent years. And with good reason – it just isn't true.

On 31 December 1998 the benchmark index of Europe's leading companies, the FTSEuroFirst 300, closed at 1182.70. Fourteen years later to the day it had fallen to 1133.96, a drop of some 4%. Over the same period any number of other asset classes, from Indonesian furniture to Central American real estate, had performed considerably better. Just how 'long term' does one have to be?

Could we not forgive the fund manager who, at this juncture, simply packed up and went home?

And yet fund managers don't pack up and go home. They stick it out, dancing like their sell-side peers to the tune of the market, waking in the dark and traipsing into work before the rest of the world has stirred.

Rightly or wrongly each believes he can make a difference, that he can out-smart the market, that bonfire of a million human emotions. Over time some do but many don't. If the experiences of the past few years have taught us anything, it is this: that making money is a good deal harder than most people appreciate.

Heads I Win, Tails You Lose:
A History Lesson

In the 1960s if you were young, talented and ambitious you went to work in journalism or in the diplomatic service. In the 1980s you dreamed of being in advertising or investment banking. In the 2000s there was only one game in town – you became a hedge-fund manager.

Once upon a time the institutional-investment world was a cottage industry and stock markets were ruled by pension-fund managers, insurance companies and banks. Neither glamorous nor flashy, they managed your money to differing degrees of success, parcelling your money into the various asset classes (mainly equities, bonds and cash) and charging a fee for doing so (in the region of 0.5–1% per annum). The authorities regulated them and smacked them on the wrist whenever they tried anything adventurous.

It wasn't exactly thrilling but no one complained – it worked.

But an investor with ability or ambition soon became frustrated. Restricted as to what he could invest in, bound in red tape and badly paid by the standards of brokers and investment bankers, he began to look for ways to spread his wings.

Hedge funds have been around since the 1960s and in some guises even earlier, but the industry began to take off only towards the end of the 1990s as an increasing number of people bought into the fantasy that hedge funds, whatever the economic conditions or market gyrations, always made money. The defining year was 2002. Stock markets, rocked by 9/11 and fearful of a worldwide meltdown, collapsed but the hedge-fund industry returned an average of 6%.

Now the genie was out of the bottle. Money began to flood into the industry, dragging with it an ever-increasing number of entrepreneurs, gluttons and chancers. Suddenly, anyone thought they could run a hedge fund. All you needed was a desk, a computer screen and a desirable address. Investment banks and broking firms were plundered for recruits, mediocre or otherwise, and doctors talked of swapping stethoscopes for securities.[21]

What on earth was going on?

Hedge funds blew traditional fee structures sky high. Many worked on a 'two and twenty' model (and indeed many still do), charging the investor a 2% annual management fee and taking 20% of any profits (in the form of a performance fee). By way of example, if a hedge fund managed (or 'ran') $500m and made a 10% return on this money, its owners would charge a management fee of $10m and would split the profits of $50m between the investors/clients (who received $40m) and themselves (who received $10m).

In other words, hedge-fund managers were using other people's money to enrich themselves beyond their wildest dreams. If they lost money it wasn't their problem – in most cases it wasn't theirs to start with. The only risk they ran was reputational.

Whichever way you look at it, it was the most brilliant get-rich-quick scheme.

In 2003–07 it was all about being in the right place at the right time. If you put up your hand and said, 'I'm a

---

21 Many of the brokers, analysts and corporate financiers who flooded into the industry during the good times are now questioning the wisdom of this decision. Some are even trying to get their old jobs back!

hedge-fund manager,' you got two and twenty, it was as simple as that. It was irrelevant whether or not you were worth it or even whether you had ever managed money before – people were too frightened of missing out on the next big thing.

The fun didn't stop there. Hedge funds were also able to use their assets as collateral and borrow money from investment banks, thereby increasing the amount of money they were able to invest (and therefore the profits they were able to make) by a multiple of the original amount. Some borrowed as much as six or seven times their original equity as banks fell over themselves to lend the money.

If we return to the example above, a hedge fund that ran $500m might borrow a further $2bn. If it made a 10% return on this revised amount (after management fees and borrowing costs), of the $250m gross profits $200m would go to the investors and $50m to the managers.

In other words, the more you borrowed the more money you made – as long as you got it right. No one stopped to consider whether a model that was, in theory, designed to align the interests of fund managers and their providers of capital was in reality encouraging excessive risk taking.

They were all too busy getting seriously rich.

Hedge funds had bucked the market trend in 2002 for the following reasons. Traditional fund managers ran 'long-only, relative return' money and their portfolios tended to follow the vagaries of the market. Many individuals had limited scope to make a difference – if they were able to 'add value' they could only nibble around the edges, their portfolios derided as little more than closet index funds (an index fund is one that exactly replicates its benchmark index). Certain managers had greater leeway but they were in the minority.

A 'LONG-ONLY' manager is one who can only bet that an asset price will rise. A 'relative return' fund is one whose performance is measured relative to the market. By way of example, if the fund falls 5% in a given year but its benchmark index (eg the FTSE100, CAC40 or Dow Jones) drops 7%, then the fund is deemed to have outperformed (or to have 'beaten the index'). An 'absolute return' fund, by contrast, aims to make money whatever the prevailing economic conditions and has as its benchmark the peer group, not a stock-market index.

Hedge funds, however, rewrote the rulebooks. They offered 'absolute return'. Largely unrestricted as to what they could invest in, they were able to operate with the kind of regulatory abandon a pension-fund manager could only dream of. Not only could they 'go short' (ie bet that an asset price would fall), they also had far greater access to derivatives, described so memorably by Warren Buffett as 'financial weapons of mass destruction'. In 2002, while traditional managers were clinging on for dear life, content to lose money as long as they outperformed the benchmark, hedge funds were making hay from the mayhem. The world could not help but sit up and take notice.[22]

---

22 A derivative (of which futures and options are both examples) is an instrument that allows an investor to bet on the direction he thinks an asset price will take and in doing so multiplies his potential risk or reward a multitude of times (often many times more than the underlying value of his assets). In 2008 the extent of their derivative exposure was enough to bring many of the world's financial institutions to their knees. Many of their bets had gone wrong, some with disastrous consequences.

And so dawned a new age of arrogance. The industry mushroomed, spawning bigger and more conceited beasts by the day. The old buy-side guard was elbowed to one side as investment banks thronged to honour the new paymasters. Hedge funds traded more regularly, more exotically and with greater intensity than the pension funds ever had. In a world awash with cheap money, they joined forces with the big banks, the sovereign wealth funds and the private equity firms to fuel an investment boom the likes of which the world had never seen.

Their tentacles spread everywhere. Tieless, ruthless and unyielding, they overturned the old orthodoxies. They bought and sold companies, both private and public, lent money, bet on takeovers, entered Hollywood and drove industry titans into retirement. 'Activist' investors and their lawyers championed the 'interests' of shareholders and forced management teams to wake from their slumbers.

But for all the charity dinners, private jets and changing of the social guard, rumblings of disquiet began to be heard. In a world of spiralling prices and closely monitored performance metrics, investors piled more and more risk onto the table, paying top dollar for assets that they couldn't sell when the tide came in and encouraging companies to load up with debt and hand back the cash to them, the shareholders. Before too long the hedge-fund industry found that it too was victim to that economic maxim, the law of diminishing returns. By 2007 the average hedge-fund manager was performing no better than his long-only counterpart. The problem was that he was charging much higher fees.

Critics soon cottoned on to another crack in the edifice. As markets headed north in 2003–07, many hedge funds did no more than replicate the investment strategies of their long-only brethren. In those sunlit days equities only ever seemed to go one way – up – and all a hedge-fund manager needed to do was buy a stock, put his feet up and watch the fees roll in. When the credit crunch arrived most investors just weren't ready for it.

The following year was cataclysmic for the industry. It might have out-performed the wider market, but in 2008 the average hedge fund returned -19%. The spell was broken. Cash-strapped banks pulled away the rug, demanding back the money they'd lent as hedge funds, already reeling from poor performance and anticipating large-scale client withdrawals, were forced to liquidate whole portfolios, driving an already petrified market deeper into the ground. Those who'd locked client money in for the long term looked on as others, regardless of performance, drowned in the quicksand, either imploding overnight or simply bleeding to death. According to Hedge Fund Research Inc, a respected industry commentator, 2008 saw 1,471 hedge funds, 15% of the total, close down.

Exit the Cavalier, Enter the Roundhead

Since then a period of much needed sobriety has followed – for obvious reasons hedge funds have been lying low. Performance since 2008 has picked up but still might be best described as patchy, and the industry has also had to watch for any regulatory brickbats that might come its way. In 2010 the European Parliament approved a new directive for hedge funds, meaning that from 2013 the industry would be subject for the first time to EU-wide regulation. While the directive intends to a) to make hedge funds more transparent by requiring them to report regularly to authorities; b) to improve the protection of underlying investors (such as pension funds); and c) to make regulation more coherent across member states, critics have seized upon it as further evidence of anti-London bias on the part of the EU (London being the place that most European hedge funds are based).

The rules aren't, however, as draconian as once feared. Hedge funds have largely escaped the caps on pay being imposed upon the wider fund management industry, and for this reason the exodus from London to countries such as Switzerland hasn't materialised in the droves first predicted. Politicians in the UK have kept pretty quiet on the subject and we shouldn't be surprised – the short-term political capital gained from bashing hedge funds pales into insignificance versus their longer-term economic benefit – and politicians on both side of the divide can ill afford to alienate the industry, however distasteful they may find some of its practices.

A more immediate consequence of the credit crunch and its aftermath has been to set the hedge-fund industry on the way to institutionalisation. Small firms are struggling to survive but the big are getting bigger. Gone are the days of twenty-seven-year-olds setting up firms in smart addresses, sourcing easy capital, buying up exotic assets and charging two and twenty for the privilege – experience, liquidity and reliability are the new watchwords. Even the great and the good find it hard to attract capital for new ventures – it's rare to read stories of hedge-fund start-ups – and fee structures are under constant pressure. These days one and ten is the new two and twenty.

In the end greater institutionalisation will lead only one way – to hedge funds behaving more like everybody else. In turn this will mean less risk, less leverage, less exoticism, less fun and lower profits. Those at the top will still be mind-bogglingly rich, but to get to the top will become that much harder. Hedge funds are here to stay but not in the way we once knew them. To the relief of wider society – if not to fund managers and all who leech off them – the era of excess and wanton abandon seems to be over.

Capital Indiscipline

Hand in hand with the hedge funds went the investment banks. If a bank wasn't lending money (as prime broker), exchanging company secrets or dictating corporate strategy (and bagging fees) on a hedge fund's behalf (see *Corporate Finance*), it was copying the way it lived and breathed.

Banks worked out some time ago that they could make more money hiring intelligent traders and entrusting them with the firm's capital than they ever could selling secondary research to the buy side. For years they racked up the profits, but when the sub-prime bubble burst they were caught in the searchlights, owners of a billion pieces of paper no one else wanted. In late 2008 most banks were bleeding so badly that senior management (with whom the buck stopped) did what they always do: they saved their own skins and closed down the problem. By Christmas that year trading floors were ghost towns and Harvard-educated whiz kids were sitting slumped in front of the tree wondering where it had all gone wrong.

Back in the 1990s prop traders sat alongside sales traders and dealers and helped them execute client business. They saw and/or anticipated the flows coming in and the flows going out and made (or lost) money off the back of them (as we saw in our earlier BP example – see *Trading*). Most hailed from the old-school fraternity – in those days prop traders had 'feel' or 'wits' or 'guts', not MBAs and undergraduate degrees – and investors were either too blind or too naive to appreciate the extent to which banks were making money at their expense.

But as hedge funds and buy-side dealers proliferated (many of whom used to work on the sell side), the investment community got wise. As more and more investors refused to have their business compromised by a bank's 'back book' (ie the capital it traded against buy-side flows), so the banks had to find a way of making money *and* keeping the client sweet. This was what prompted them to set up other prop books (essentially internal hedge funds with hedge-fund fee structures) and segregate them off (behind Chinese Walls) from the client-facing, flow-based prop activities that would now exist primarily to serve the client.[23] 'Pure' (ie segregated) prop traders would cross over to the buy side and would analyse companies, patronise brokers and bow down to bankers along with every other commission-paying investor.

This precipitated a free-for-all. Although prop was starved of its lifeblood (client trade flows) and the edge it afforded, it no longer carried a social stigma. Two and twenty was the new game in town and everyone wanted a piece. Banks packed off their most talented analysts, brokers and traders to the prop desks, reasoning that it made good sense to put the brightest and best in charge of the vault. Unlike hedge funds and their myriad clients, a prop book had one master – the bank – to keep sweet. If it liked what you were doing – and in those early days everyone made money – then the drip-drip-drip of capital was incessant. Some banks were making so much money that they revolutionised the way they did business, getting analysts to serve the prop book first and the client a distant second.

In other words, they became giant hedge funds.

For everyone concerned, it was a golden age. In a world

---

23 But let's be under no illusions – banks will very rarely offer a loss-making service if they can at all avoid it.

where asset prices only ever seemed to rise, it was like hitting blackjack every time. The more money you made the more money you got to play with, and as long as you made money, controls were lax and risk assessment seemingly non-existent. A commodities trader at a leading investment bank best summed it up when he said,

'If I make money [in a given year] then they pay me a fixed percentage of my profits. If I lose money then they still pay me a million dollars. Only if I lose money a second time will they ever fire me.'

In other words, you could bet the bank, get it wrong and still not get fired, what those in the industry might term 'a free call' or the man in the street a 'get-out-of-jail-free card'. Even if you got it wrong and were given the boot, you could always return to less glamorous but hardly dowdy pursuits like equity sales or research.

If, on the other hand, you got it right then the rewards were obscene. No wonder everyone went to town.

MOST MEMBERS OF Senior Management/Compliance sat back and let prop traders get on with it. They were either a) too gullible and/or too timid to pay much attention, more likely to beg a trader to 'take care' than to poke their noses into his business (as long as a trader talked a cautious game he'd be left well alone) or b) complicit in the scam and getting too rich to want to rock the boat. Shareholders took no notice either – they were too busy counting the profits to wish to know how they were made.

2008, however, saw an exodus as rapid as the foray had been frenzied. Markets collapsed and performance sagged. As prop books were liquidated and traders lined up in the streets to be shot, management and their cronies in Compliance went out of their way to say 'I told you so'. If public vitriol was reserved for 'bankers', a generic term if ever there was one, the City was more discerning, pointing the finger at both the creators of Armageddon (the rocket scientists behind credit derivatives *et al*) and its financiers (investment banks, hedge funds and anyone else who lent or borrowed money).

But as the autumn of 2008 led into the winter of 2008 and banks packed up their prop desks and vowed 'never again', some were back at the coalface, pouring capital into places others had but recently abandoned. One look at the Goldman Sachs numbers for 2009 will tell you all you need to know about the City's capacity for reinvention and its never-ending thirst for self-enrichment. For all the talk about regulatory reform and slashing bonuses, banks exist to make money, and making money is all about risking capital in areas no one else dares attack. As Warren Buffett once said, 'We simply attempt to be fearful when others are greedy and to be greedy only when others are fearful'.

In other words, once the dust has settled and the new parameters have been established, risk taking will be back on the agenda. Quite simply, banks can't bear to miss out on a party. When they get it right they make serious money from prop.

$

WHAT THOSE PARAMETERS will be is still anyone's guess. Where prop is concerned confusion now reigns supreme. Attempts have been made in the US (led by former US Federal Reserve Chairman Paul Volcker) to introduce legislation banning commercial banks from proprietary trading, but the proposals have met with opposition from a variety of parties, from banks claiming they're too costly to implement to reform advocates berating their many loopholes. Something will be done but as yet no one knows what. In the end it will come down to definition and/or legitimacy – what counts ultimately as 'prop' will be banned and what doesn't will be safe (and this will differ by both jurisdiction and asset class). Some investment banks are already taking no chances and are busy folding pure prop departments into their flow-based brethren, spinning them off into fund-management divisions or renaming them as something less exotic. Others are watching and waiting for the final outcome, their prop activities essentially frozen in limbo.

Sparring with the Sell Side

While most fund managers will arrive by the time the market opens at 8am, some keep irregular and often eccentric hours, claiming to do their best thinking away from the distractions of the office. A number of fund managers will look for any excuse to skive off work. Some claim to be 'working from home' while others are more inventive – playing tennis and bird watching are both popular pastimes. To what extent you have similar latitude will depend on your experience or on your track record. Those without either can expect to put in a full day's shift.

As we have already seen, brokers, traders and analysts emerge from their morning meetings and bombard the investment community with a blizzard of calls and emails. By the time you arrive at your desk and turn on your computer, a wealth of information will be waiting for you, all condensed and packaged to your taste. Imagine sitting down in a restaurant and watching as the waiters rush to bring food to your table. You'll accept some dishes and refuse others, gratifying your favourite waiters with a smile and a generous tip. Brokers are like waiters – they clamour for your attention and compete to drown you in their synopses of, and reactions to, that morning's news.

How much notice you take is up to you. In the early days you'll be more assiduous, keen to impress your superiors and at pains to embrace every fact, however unnecessary or irrelevant it might first appear. Later on, however, you will be more discriminating, having learned what to look for and what to disregard.

$

> OLDER FUND MANAGERS often combine greater discrim-
> ination with a lower degree of enthusiasm – with
> experience come both acuity and indolence. Some have
> made their mark (and their money) and are simply more
> relaxed, while others are freewheeling, doing no more than
> going through the motions.

Let's now have a look at some of the conversations a broker or analyst might have with a fund manager, this time from the latter's perspective.

a) Receive/make a call about a stock/sector you have been following.

If one of your stocks is in the news then you'll have to be on your toes. At this stage having a healthy relationship with the sell side can be invaluable. If a broker or analyst calls you and says,

'You're a holder of DIY Deluxe, aren't you? The numbers this morning are shocking. We'll be downgrading earnings [profits] by around 10%.'

Or

'Our analyst reckons these numbers from Organic Food King look pretty dreary. Like-for-like sales have been disappointing. We'd be selling the stock and switching into Tesco. We think it's attractive at these levels.'

Or

'Are you guys still short the retailers? We think the sell-off's gone far enough. Metro's comments this morning make an excellent read-across for the rest of the sector.'

You'll begin to get a feel for how the market might respond to what a company has announced that morning. Of course you might be more than capable of interpreting the announcement for yourself, but most people take comfort from knowing what the market (or the 'street') is saying. It means you can go into the morning meeting and speak to your colleagues with the requisite authority. Having the broking community on your side is like going into an exam with your revision notes tucked under your arm.

AT THE START of your career you won't be ready to manage money or make investment decisions. Instead you will be assigned an analytical role (where you can expect to spend at least three years), charged with appraising your more senior colleagues as to the fortunes of the companies under your jurisdiction. In the major equity markets there are some 20 sectors and you will be responsible for ten or so stocks in a given sector. Although each sector can comprise anywhere between 5 and 50 companies, you need have knowledge of only the most important.

b) Call your favourite broker but ignore all the others.

At this hour of the morning broking firms are reacting to that day's company announcements and hence tend to repeat each other. If you want a morning round-up but don't want to be plagued by a myriad of different brokers, then choose one you like and ask that he or she calls you just before the market opens. That way you'll be up to speed with events whether you're in bed, at the gym or at your desk. You can then ignore your telephone, safe in the knowledge that you have most things you need.

$

> SOME FUND MANAGERS take broker-avoidance measures to an extreme, refusing to communicate with them under any circumstances. As many of them used to be brokers, they're well placed to assess the sell side's shortcomings. Ex-brokers can make the most unpleasant fund managers. It's all about revenge – spending years on the wrong end of the telephone is enough to drive anyone to distraction.

On certain occasions, however, brokers will have something specific to discuss, such as a share placing or an IPO, and will need to be able to get hold of you. If you let them, a broker will always have ways of tracking you down and you'll soon learn which firms you cannot do without.

If a broker calls you and says,

'We're placing [ie selling a stake worth] $300m of Vodafone this morning – do you want any?'

You'll need to react quickly, particularly if your firm is interested and there's demand for the stock. Other situations require less speedy responses but are still worthy of your attention.

'Hey there – we're doing an IPO I think you'll be interested in. Do you have a spare couple of minutes?'

It's then up to you whether you take the conversation further. Much of the time investors will agree to have a look at the latest (dubious) investment offering just to get the broker off the phone.

> IF YOU HATE being hassled by brokers then you might prefer to work in the US, where a fund manager rarely if ever picks up his phone. Instead, brokers will leave pre-rehearsed messages on your answerphone that you can listen to at your leisure (if indeed you choose to – many don't).

c) Bribe the broker.

If you can flash the cash then you should – in this game money buys you friends and friends get you information. If you call a broker and say,

'I've got some business for you. Please do these trades.'

And then you add,

'By the way, I need you to do something for me. Can you find out what's really going on in the steel sector? I've been hearing some bid talk.'

The broker will go to the ends of the earth for you, however tiresome the request. Having a broker on side can confer other advantages. He'll sing your praises to his superiors, thereby raising your profile and affording you better treatment where IPOs and placings are concerned (ie you should receive more stock than your peers).

> SOME INVESTORS ARE brilliant at securing a broker's
> life-long loyalty for a pittance. If you meet a broker whom
> you like and whose services you wish to encourage, it
> makes sense to hook him early on – brokers soon
> grow bored of clients who promise much but offer little.
> Front-loading his commission and then fading it to
> a more realistic level will ensnare him for ever – he'll
> keep calling in the hope that one day he'll land another
> jumbo payday.

d) Call up a broker/analyst and sell him your ideas/find out what your peers are up to.

Investors love to know a) what everyone else is doing and b) how they're performing. The industry has an obsession with league tables and statistics that puts many a professional sport to shame. Performance data is published on a daily basis and fund managers fight tooth and nail to get hold of each other's monthly newsletters, desperate to glean the nugget of an idea or to gloat over another's misfortune.

Where data is less readily available, fund managers will happily mislead each other as to the quality or otherwise of their performance. They will either lie (eg claiming they're up 15% when they're really up 5% – actual individual performance can be very hard to quantify, especially in a fund managed by two people or more) or be creative with the truth (eg tell the truth and say they're up 15% but not explain the horrific risks they ran to get there). It's a sad but incontestable fact that many a social gathering is still dominated by talk such as 'Have you heard how well Hamish is performing?' or 'How does Pierre keep hold of his job? Has he ever made anyone any money?'

This is an industry that relies heavily on plagiarism. Some steal ideas discreetly while others are more blatant. 'Borrowing' someone else's ideas is quite legitimate and often encouraged – a fund manager likes nothing more than to earn the idolatry of his peers.[24]

Using a broker or an analyst as your agent is the best way both to promote your own ideas and to filch other people's.

'By the way, have a look at Western Power. I've done some work on the balance sheet and the interest charge is going through the roof. Why don't you guys write a note on it?'

Or

'Is it true that Patrick is still playing the inflation trade? Can you send me his latest newsletter?'

Brokers and analysts will always be happy to oblige if you let them into your conspiracy. You are their master and they seek your favour.

e) Call a broker and pretend to be his friend.

Some fund managers are the most shameless scroungers. This suits the sell-side community, many of whom are shamelessly disingenuous. The City is full of people pretending to be each other's friends, seducing each other with promises of sports tickets and commission.

'Hey mate, don't know if you can get hold of any tickets to Barca–Real this weekend? I'd love to take my son along.'

---

24 It's all to do with the timing. If a fund manager is buying a stock and you join the fray before he has finished building his stake, he won't thank you if you help push the price up into the stratosphere. By contrast, if he has the position he desires and you come along and inflate the price, then he'll be delighted!

'Let me see what I can do. I'll try and pull a few strings.'

'Nice one. Let me know. Buy me $10m worth of HSBC in here, will you?'

Or

'I see the new Marco Pierre White restaurant has had brilliant reviews. Shall we take the girls along?'

'Good idea. I'll try and book the chef's table.'

'Awesome. Sell me some France Telecom, will you? I've got 300,000 to go.'

However much money they make for themselves, fund managers seem to have insatiable appetites for nights out at other people's expense. In the heady days of 2003–07, client entertainment reached dizzying heights as hedge-fund commission ballooned and broking firms battled it out for the spoils. Nowhere was off limits as fund managers were feted like rock stars and enjoyed more freebies than the average politician. These days it still happens but to a much lesser extent and what goes on is far less blatant. Brokers are under pressure to justify everything to their superiors while fund managers have to limit what they receive to avoid a) being obligated to brokers they cannot repay and b) falling foul of bribery legislation. Largesse will return, of course. It always does. After all, it makes good business sense and it's not your money!

f) Give a broker a hard time for getting something wrong.

Even though the buck always stops with you, it's easier to blame the broker if the two of you conspire to lose money.

If he calls you and says,

'Bank of Irrelevance has got numbers tomorrow. I think the stock's looking oversold.'

You might reply,

'That's a good idea. I think I'll have a few.'

If the stock then goes in the wrong direction, you've got three choices. You can point the finger at him and say,

'What the hell were you thinking of? Get me out before you lose me any more money!'

Or (if you're feeling more reasonable),

'The impairment charge was always going to be shocking. Don't worry about it – these things happen.'

Or you can leave him sweating and wait for him to grovel. When he finally gets hold of you, you accept his apology and tell him you closed the position first thing that morning. If you didn't give his firm the trade and he's the paranoid sort (most brokers are), he'll spend the rest of the day wondering how far he's slipped in your estimation and how he can make it up to you. Losing money doesn't always have to be to your disadvantage.

g) Give a broker a hard time for *not* telling you something.

Sparks can fly when a self-important investor doesn't get the service he feels he deserves. It doesn't always follow that the broker is negligent – he might be genuinely unaware that his client is following a certain stock or situation.

'Why the FUCK haven't you called me on Michelin? You should know we care about this one. The stock's through the roof and I haven't got a clue what's going on. What's your analyst saying?'

If the broker has any sense he'll run off and find out what's going on. Some, however, will try to brazen it out, scrolling desperately through their emails as the client fumes on the other end of the phone.

h) Make money by spreading false rumours.

Hedge-fund managers are past masters at buying and selling stocks through one broker and then getting another to boost or trash the share price.

'Do you know if there's any truth in the rumour that's doing the rounds? We're hearing that the Chinese move for BHP is back on.'

The idea is that as the second broker rings around his contacts to ascertain the truth the share price moves in the desired direction.

'We're hearing that the BHP deal is back on. I don't know if you've heard anything but it's probably worth having a few just to be on the safe side.'

Many fund managers will take the bait – they love rumours and hate missing out on the next big thing. By the time the story reaches the furthest investor outpost the story will have been discredited and you will be long gone (ideally with a healthy profit).

In the pre-crunch days this game was commonly played on a Friday. In firms across the City brokers, traders and fund managers would ask,

'Why has Ladbrokes just spiked 10%?'

and when they received the reply,

'There's a bid rumour. It's Friday.'

some would nod and return to whatever they'd been doing, as unflustered as a man who hears a lunatic is at large but that the police are hot on his heels. Others, however, would be unable to restrain themselves and would rush to buy the stock (in this world a pessimist is a rarity). And, as they did so, a fund manager and his friends would be pocketing a fortune, sitting back and looking forward to another excellent weekend.

i) Ignore messages from brokers telling you things you don't want to know.

Many brokers operate a scattergun policy to contacting fund managers. As well as phone calls and emails, a broker can deploy the torpedo known as the Bloomberg message. As well as providing you with every conceivable piece of financial information, your Bloomberg terminal also provides you with a messaging function. When a broker types your name into the message box the colour of the dot by your name signifies immediately whether or not you are in the office – green means you're there, amber that you're there but away from your desk and red that you're AWOL.[25]

Sending a Bloomberg message is a great way for a broker to a) avoid having to make a phone call, b) reach a wide variety of clients at the same time and c) contact a client

---

25 Certain individuals choose to deploy a grey dot – this tells other people that they have a 'private' account and don't wish to alert others as to their availability or otherwise.

on a subject he may have no interest in while avoiding being told to get lost. For example, if you cover European retail stocks and you receive the message,

'Morning, Adrian [this is probably not your name. The broker is so slapdash and/or negligent that he's cut and pasted the message several times over without changing any of the personal details]. We think the Japanese tech sector looks excellent value. Have a look at Sony and Panasonic – both are trading one standard deviation below trend PE. We'd go long these and short[26] SAP against them'.

or

'These Total numbers are 5% ahead of our expectations. They're talking a big game on upstream capex – we'd be buying into the likes of Schlumberger',

you'll know immediately that the broker hasn't done his homework where you are concerned (or on many other investors for that matter – you might all have received the same nonsense).

The easiest thing to do is to ignore all future messages from that particular broker. This doesn't mean he'll back off – some broking firms/sales teams are renowned for their (pig-headed) persistence.

---

26 Hedge funds have a number of tricks up their sleeves if they want to bet against a rising market. 'Shorting' a stock is probably the best known and most infamous tactic. In essence an investor 'borrows' stock from another investor and sells it, hoping to be able later on to buy it back at a lower price, return it to its rightful owner and book a profit. Short selling worked brilliantly in the aftermath of 9/11 as stock markets collapsed but came in for heavy criticism as the credit crunch unfolded. The share prices of many financial stocks nosedived as investors bet – wrongly in many cases – on widespread insolvency, and in certain jurisdictions (such as Italy) the authorities were forced to stem the panic by stepping in and banning short selling altogether.

j) Have the broker persuade you to do something you didn't think you wanted to do.

The best brokers are those who can get their clients to do things the client doesn't necessarily want to do. In the City the importance of distribution is paramount, particularly in the eyes of investment bankers.

For example, if a broking firm has an IPO or a placing that might prove tricky then its sales team will need to pull out the stops. Most deals fall into this category – they're never as wonderful as capital-markets departments claim, and investors look for any excuse to avoid them.

'You've got to have some of the placing we're doing in Cosmic Caravans. Trust me on this one – the company's not telling you the full story. They've got contracts coming out of their ears.'

'I'm not convinced but if you need me to help out then I will. Put me down for $2m.'

Some brokers have the knack of blowing a client up in one deal while talking him into the next. Ultimately the City is a people business – the value of a good address book cannot be overstated.

Morning Glory

The morning meeting is the time when a firm's investment professionals sit down and grapple with the implications of that morning's news. Most days will be humdrum and routine, but every so often something momentous takes place. By any standards, 2008 was an extraordinary year – on a weekly basis investors would arrive at work and be greeted with an event of dizzying significance. Whether it was the nationalisation of Freddie Mac and Fannie Mae, the collapse of Lehman Brothers or the short squeeze in

Volkswagen, investors were wrestling with issues and circumstances that they would expect to encounter no more than two or three times in a whole career.

In most firms the meeting takes place at around 8.30am GMT. By that time the market will have been trading for half an hour and share prices will have had time to react to any morning announcements or to overnight moves in international markets (such as the US and Japan). Most days a variety of companies will say something of note. Announcements will either be scheduled (such as a profits release or a trading update) or unscheduled (such as a takeover approach or – the thing feared by all fund managers, unless they are 'short' – a profit warning, ie a statement that profits are going to be worse than the market expects). Profit warnings tend to trigger a collapse in a company's share price.

Sometimes the way in which a stock behaves can confound even the experts. You might think it obvious that a share price will rise or fall on a certain announcement, but stocks can act in unpredictable ways. For example, a company might put out a statement saying that profits have collapsed and will now be half the level everyone was expecting and the stock, while starting the day down 20%, will be up 5% by midday and finish the day higher still.[27] Nowhere is the cliché 'information is power' more apt than in the City. Investors will fight tooth and tail (by fair means and foul) to be the first to find out the truth – indeed it's quite normal for a company to say something that comes as little or no surprise to whole swaths of the buy-side community.

---

27 This can happen for any number of reasons. Sometimes the company will reveal things over the course of the day that cause investors and analysts to revise their views, and on other occasions the news reported that morning will already have been factored in (or 'discounted') by the share price.

Fund managers and corporate financiers have always had a mutual affinity. Investors have ideas that bankers can put to good (ie fee-generating) use, while bankers can talk companies into deals that they claim to be in the best interests of shareholders. To the investor a well-informed/well-connected banker is worth his weight in gold, but things can get too cosy. During 2003–07 people began to wonder to what extent corporate financiers might be in the pay or under the sway of unscrupulous investors, and in 2007 the UK authorities were alleged to have investigated around one third of London Stock Exchange trades in stocks that were subsequently bid for.

Although one would like to believe that most investors weren't so lacking in scruples, in those days it was extraordinary just how many stocks leapt hours or even minutes before they were bid for. The reality is that confidential information can leak from any number of sources – bankers, lawyers, accountants, printers or company boards/management teams. We'll have more on this in the next chapter – see *Corporate Finance* – but, try as you might, you'll never keep everyone's mouths shut. As the chatterboxes know only too well, establishing proof in such situations is notoriously difficult, whatever the authorities might be doing these days to shore up any leaks.

In the morning meeting – if it's a large firm – it's not uncommon for the big cheeses (the old, red-faced fund managers) to assume seats around the table while the junior analysts stand or sit on the floor. The analysts will say their bit and then the more niggardly fund managers will try to pick holes in their arguments. As in the real world, the laws of the jungle apply – it's no different from watching nature programmes where old male gorillas take swipes at their younger rivals.

Although you might come to appreciate it for the theatre it is, being on the receiving end yourself is no fun at all. If you say,

'Transatlantic Air has put out a pretty lacklustre statement this morning. They're talking about falling yields on their premium routes. I think we should be selling our position.'

One of your colleagues might reply,

'I absolutely disagree. This is hardly new news – we've known this for ages. A couple of the others said the same thing last month. If the stock's weak on this we should be buying more – it's only going to revive the consolidation rumours.'

And if you say,

'There's a rumour of a bid approach for Electrolux. They haven't confirmed it yet but the stock is up 10% this morning. I think we should take the money and run',

you might be shot down with,

'What complete crap. If it's true there'll be several bidders in the frame. We should sit tight and wait.'

As a young analyst you face the same problems that young brokers do – you lack experience. What might seem to be the most brilliant observation can be shot down in flames by a colleague with a longer memory and/or a desire for the limelight. During the early days, even if you're convinced you're right, it's better to profess the most anodyne of opinions and leave others to make the mistakes.

SOME FUND MANAGERS are quite happy to bluff their way through meetings in the manner of brokers or traders. Ever loath to show themselves at a loss, they'll make up all manner of facts or statistics, safe in the knowledge that most people are unlikely and/or insufficiently spiteful to go away and check.

Trouble and Strife

The rise of the hedge fund engendered an abundance of weird and wonderful investment strategies. No longer did investors manage bread-and-butter portfolios which more or less mirrored the major stock-market indices. No longer was it a straight choice between 'value', 'growth' and 'income'.[28] Gone were the days of buying a stock and holding it for several years. In the brave new world investors were in and out of stocks by lunchtime, dabbling in distressed debt and derivatives and claiming to be 'long-short', 'risk-arb', 'event driven', 'market neutral', 'global macro' or anything else they happened to fancy. Some funds even got rid of the human element altogether, preferring to entrust their investment decisions to computer-based models in a strategy known as 'quant investing'. Unfortunately, in 2007-08 the playing field became so crowded that many of the more sophisticated strategies became some of the worst performing. Their authors had assumed that markets would always behave in predictable ways.[29]

28 In a nutshell, 'value' investing is all about finding stocks that look under-valued or unloved, 'growth' investing is what it says on the tin (ie identifying growing companies) and 'income' fund managers are attracted to stocks that pay dividends.

29 2009 saw a rash of articles on the death of the 'efficient markets hypothesis'. For most of the last century academics and economists had regarded markets as self-correcting, that is not prone to irrational extremes of emotion, a myth debunked by the collapse of Lehman Brothers and the chaos that ensued.

Your fund's strategy will go a long way towards dictating how you make investment decisions. In many cases you'll be trying to ascertain a company's holistic merits or to establish whether you or your colleagues should buy or sell the shares, but in some firms you'll be looking for something more specific, such as the probability of one stock making a bid for another, the effect that a restructuring measure might have on a company's fortunes or the likely direction of an asset price over the course of the next two hours.

Depending on your firm's size and the way it is structured, you will either manage your own portfolio or share responsibilities with a number of other people. Many funds are specific in their aims (such as 'smaller company growth' or 'clean technology'), while others are more amorphous ('pan European long short') and hence have the scope to dirty their hands in practically anything their managers choose. The hedge-fund crashes of 2008 were exacerbated by the fact that many funds were sitting on unquoted, esoteric assets that had collapsed in value and for which there were no buyers. Back in the good old days these assets had multiplied several times over and were the drivers behind many investors' stellar returns. In 2008, fund managers had to raise cash quickly and were forced to sell their better performing, more liquid stocks, thereby driving each and every share price down into the ground.

Some firms are nimble and make decisions on the spot, while others are painstaking and ponderous and take an age to do anything. Red tape can demand that every single box is ticked before an investment decision is made (such as meeting the company and getting consent from every relevant member of the team), and people delight in disagreeing with each other for the sake of disagreeing. Although there's much to be said for collective responsibility, on many occasions it's an excuse for pedantry.

'Are we sure we want to do this? There's something I don't trust about a man with a beard.'

Riding alone, on the other hand, is great when things go well, but be warned – many investors don't enjoy restful existences. Some eat, drink and sleep the job to the point of distraction, unable to unplug themselves from the stresses of managing millions, if not billions, of dollars of other people's money. An anxious fund manager is no fun to be around – he has eyes only for the market – and people soon get the hint. Even on holiday his eyes will be glued to the screen and not to the ski slopes. Some watch their lives unravel around them, helpless as they obliterate address books and love lives. One well-known fund manager claims that he has 'neither the time nor the energy to take girls on dates'.

Now while fund managers will spend much of their time staring transfixed as share prices yo-yo up and down on their screens, behaviour as compulsive as playing fruit machines in an arcade, there'll be occasions when they return to earth and seek your opinion. If you're the retail-sector analyst, for example, and cover JD Sports, a colleague might want to know how much the company's profits will be affected as more sales migrate to the internet, a scenario he believes will arise. You'll then have to weigh up the different variables and arrive at a conclusion.

How you come to this conclusion is up to you. You might have most of the information at your fingertips, but in the likely event that you don't then you'll need to find someone who does.

The most obvious solution is 1), to phone an analyst covering JD Sports at a broking firm and ask for his opinion. You might even request that he sends you his financial model, thereby saving you both time and aggravation. If you are particularly virtuous you might contact more than one sell-side analyst or broker, ask for each of their models and compare and contrast the answers.

A more laborious exercise is 2), to contact the company directly and request their assistance. Some companies, however, can be obtuse in the extreme and will only answer your questions or return your call if you happen to hail from one of the major investment firms. Many companies hide behind the excuse of being in a 'quiet period', a time between results releases when they're obliged not to say anything of a 'price sensitive' nature. How discreet the company is depends on the country you're dealing with. Most UK companies adopt the attitude of a prim and matronly aunt, refusing to flout the rules and say anything that might be construed as interesting. The French and Germans, by contrast, are only too willing to spill the beans, happy to tell you everything and anything.

Many buy-side analysts choose option 3), which is to call up a favoured analyst or broker and get him to do their dirty work for them, such as asking questions of the company and/or crunching any numbers. This way they get to put their feet up and pass off someone else's opinions as their own.

Once you've done all this you can then report back to the fund manager and relay your conclusions. If he decides to follow your advice you might ask him to 'direct a trade' – ie buy or sell shares in JD Sports via the broking firm that has been most helpful, thereby ensuring that the broker gets paid for his work.[30]

Fund managers don't spend all day staring at screens or poring over spreadsheets. Provided you're not being badgered by brokers or indulging in some other trifle, there are things you might be getting on with. One option is to invite a sell-side analyst to come in and showcase his favourite ideas/talk through a theme/stock in which you are interested. Alternatively, you might attend a company presentation or an analyst/capital-markets day (where companies spend all day telling you how wonderful they are and sell-side analysts queue up to agree).

While some investors relish savaging analysts as much as they enjoy patronising brokers, others look forward to these visits with as much enthusiasm as a trip to the dentist. Analysts take an equally jaundiced view – such occasions are either a waste of their valuable time (and won't the broker know it!) or a trip to the lion's den where they'll maul or be mauled.

FOR THE BROKER it's as painful to witness a client toy with an analyst as it is to watch an analyst lord his way through a meeting. In fact, it's hard to know which is worse – a discredited analyst brings shame on the firm but an ineffectual client calls the broker's standing into doubt. Mediocre clients normally talk to mediocre brokers. It's not unusual for a fund manager to call his broker after a meeting has taken place and say, 'Just who was that idiot? He was absolutely bloody clueless. Don't ever bring him round again!'

---

30 However – see *Trading* – getting a broker to help you doesn't mean you have to pay him. You can overlook him for any number of reasons, even if it makes him less inclined to assist you in the future. Your dealing colleagues might prefer to use another broker to execute the trade or you might simply choose to be perverse.

Most days company management teams will visit your offices – gauging the success or otherwise of a company meeting is a key part of a fund manager's job (some investors will meet as many as 300 companies over a 12-month period). If you're going to invest in a business then knowing who runs it and establishing whether or not they're worth backing is critical. Some long-only funds place particular emphasis on these meetings, with fund managers prohibited from investing in a stock unless they have met its management on at least one occasion. This can be frustrating for brokers who introduce an idea but fail to see their client act on it until it's too late – by the time the investor meets the management the share price may have already moved too far in the desired direction.

How fund managers approach these meetings depends on who's coming in to see them. If the company is blue-chip royalty then investors will fawn and swoon, wearing glassy grins and sucking up to the management in the manner of star-struck adolescents.

'I'd just like to say what a wonderful job you've done in keeping costs under control. Could you spend a few minutes telling us how you did it?'

Or

'Your domestic performance has been quite stunning. Has it exceeded even your high expectations?'

But if the company is from the lower reaches of society or if your firm is an unhappy shareholder, then the approach can be quite different. Some investors will be difficult and others downright rude, indifferent as to what the company has to say and intent on demonstrating how intelligent they are.

'You claimed you had pricing power but you patently don't. Why should we believe anything you say?'

Or

'Can we talk a little bit more about your strategy? I'm not sure you understand what you're trying to achieve.'

Much of the time fund managers drift through company meetings without incident, but there are times you'll want to have a ringside seat. We can only begin to imagine the sparks that would have flown in 2012 between the management of Barclays and their leading shareholders as news of the Libor scandal broke.

To what extent a company's fortunes rest on the abilities of its senior executives is a matter for debate. Depending on whom you ask, management teams are either cut-and-paste automata or integral cogs in the corporate wheel. It tends to follow that the smaller the business the more crucial the quality of its executives – small/young companies are more vulnerable to being hijacked by fantasists who have little regard for other shareholders. Fund managers have to take especial care with these businesses – there are countless examples of very experienced investors being led up very long garden paths to find nothing but a chimera at the end.

Many blue-chip corporations are run by grey-suited executives whose faces all blur into the same indistinguishable fug. In a famous example of fund-manager confusion, the chairman of a leading European company was told that he 'made a welcome change from his idiotic predecessor' (whom the fund manager had met a year earlier). The chairman managed a wry smile but neglected to say that nothing had in fact changed at the top – in the intervening year his aristocratic father had died and he had inherited his title!

> MORE OFTEN THAN not the company management will be accompanied by a broker. As we have already seen, the broker doesn't do much more than sit there and smile nicely, his role no more grandiose than that of a wet nurse. Broking firms like to have representatives in such meetings as it a) keeps them close to both the company and the investor, b) ensures that their man is the first to hear anything important and c) acts as a muzzle on management in case they say anything stupid. Some fund managers, however, bar brokers from their meetings, believing (quite rightly) that a chief executive is more likely to speak his mind if a broker isn't there.

For a long time managers of the larger, better-established companies had it easy. They enjoyed cosy relationships with their long-term shareholders, the pension funds and insurance companies, and could more or less act with impunity. These shareholders would sanction the most hare-brained of their strategic ideas, waving through acquisitions, disposals and pay rises with the equanimity of a man drinking champagne on a sun-streaked beach. Shareholders did not vote against resolutions – abstention was the extent of their ire.

Hedge funds, however, put a stop to that, taking stakes in companies and agitating for change (which in the real world translates as getting companies to save money by sacking their staff – a favourite private equity trick – see *Corporate Finance*). They didn't even need to build large stakes – the publicity alone was sufficient to wake management teams from their slumber. If an executive made a false move, a shareholder could topple him with a peashooter. In a sign of how ridiculous things were becoming, a hedge fund might take a tiny stake in a multinational company and kick up a fuss. Activist investor Knight Vinke, for example, was for some time engaged in a battle with HSBC despite holding less than 1% of the equity.

Some of the most spectacular bust-ups of recent years occurred as hedge funds pulled one way and management teams the other. If TCI captured the headlines with its twin assaults upon ABN Amro and Deutsche Börse[31], there were numerous other examples of hedge funds taking stakes in companies and training their sights on management. On many occasions disputes were resolved amicably to the benefit of everyone, but there were times when investor egotism crashed headlong into management intransigence. Some management teams, running in fear for their professional lives, would go so far as to refuse to see certain funds and would badmouth them to all and sundry.

Although the credit crunch and the turmoil it engendered caused most activist investors to down tools and slip away to lick their wounds (in some cases never to return), there have been signs more recently that activism is back on the agenda, albeit with greater emphasis on pragmatism and less on confrontation for confrontation's sake. Pay, performance and corporate governance have all been in the spotlight as pension funds and insurance companies finally learn to follow the hedge funds' lead and take a stand. The so-called 'shareholder spring' of 2012 saw shareholders rise up in rebellion at companies as diverse

---

31 The most cited example of hedge-fund duress was the resignation of Deutsche Börse CEO Werner Seifert in 2007 after pressure from London-based The Children's Investment Fund (TCI). This led to Franz Müntefering, Chairman of the German Social Democratic Party, accusing TCI of behaving like 'locusts'.

as Yahoo!, Aviva and Unilever, to name but three, and as long as economic uncertainties remain we should expect executives and their boards to be in for an uncomfortable ride. However what happens in the longer-term remains to be seen. History tells us that we shouldn't count our chickens where the long-only fraternity and activism are concerned.

Star Wars

Once upon a time there was little glamour in fund management. Investors did not adorn the front covers of magazines or feature in the gossip columns. Today, however, things are quite different. Fund management has embraced celebrity culture, and with that comes all the squabbling, self-regard and narcissism that we encounter every day in the tabloid press.

A handful of investors saw the credit crunch coming and emerged with their reputations enhanced.[32] These stars are an eclectic bunch – they can be charming and charismatic, or can border on the autistic. What they have in common is a) foresight, b) the courage of their convictions (especially when flying in the face of popular wisdom) and c) an emotional detachment from companies and the people who run them – a good fund manager is one who knows when to offload a stock he loves.

Star names are always conscious of where they rank in the pantheon. While the rise of the hedge fund and ensuing proliferation of different strategies has muddied the water

---

32 Notable among them was US investor John Paulson. He foresaw the sub-prime fiasco as early as 2005 and hit the jackpot when the storm broke, netting a return of 590% in 2007 and pocketing $15bn in profits for himself and his clients. He later told the *Wall Street Journal* that 'I've never been involved in a trade that had such unlimited upside with a very limited downside'.

as to who sits in front of whom (because we're no longer comparing apples with apples), there's an unofficial ranking system with managers being promoted or relegated according to their fortunes. On certain occasions, such as at a company conference or at a sporting event, you might be lucky enough to witness two members of the elite cross paths. Watch for the exaggerated politeness and faux bonhomie as they eye each other with the wary respect of a bull and a toreador.

Of course, star names don't always get it right, and following one into a stock that collapses won't do you any favours either. Justifying your investment decision on the basis that X or Y made the same mistake won't cut any ice with your boss or your own investors. Some star names spend an age in the wilderness, prepared to blot their copybooks for years on end in an attempt to prove their genius.[33]

If you're not a star name yourself then it's quite possible you'll be working for one. While such an association is normally to your advantage, a good investor doesn't necessarily make a good boss – many stars are so cocooned inside their own egos that they can neglect and/or obstruct those whom they employ. In this way they're no less self-centred than their managerial counterparts on the sell side.

Stars differ as to the extent they allow others to have their say. Some are tyrants, reluctant to let a pin drop without their permission, while others are more laissez-faire,

---

33 Perhaps the most famous example was that of the late Tony Dye, Chief Investment Officer of Phillips and Drew. Known as 'Dr Doom', he refused to buy into the bull market of the late 1990s, shunning growth stocks and moving large amounts of money out of the market and into cash. His controversial approach lost him both friends and investors, and he was sacked in February 2000 just weeks before markets hit their all-time highs.

happy to farm out responsibility to those they consider most deserving of their trust.

Many stars have protégés who go on to become as famous as their mentors. These relationships are often fraught with complication – stars don't want to be superseded by subordinates any more than protégés want to be restrained by their mentors (especially if they think they can do a better job). The hedge-fund boom of 2003–07 accelerated as managers jumped ship and firms splintered into newer, smaller entities. Although managers went their own way for a variety of reasons, in most cases money was at the root of the break-up, with protégés taking the view that it made no sense to view two and twenty from half way down the food chain if you could view it from the peak. Some soon found that life wasn't so easy on their own and scurried back to the mother ship, only to find the door had been bolted and they were now deemed surplus to requirements!

$

SOME FUND MANAGERS, especially those close to but not at the very top, indulge in the most shameless self-promotion and take every opportunity to broadcast their opinions across every available medium. However their efforts don't always have the desired effect. One fund manager made the mistake of appearing on a flagship TV news programme without having first done his homework. Under the impression he was there to talk about nothing other than his equity portfolio, he began to flounder when the interviewer – politely but insistently – pressed him upon the subject of Greek credit default swaps. As he played for time and tried to deflect the question, the interviewer cut him off in his prime, citing technical issues. Suffice to say, the fund manager was never asked to return.

Investors come in as many shapes and sizes as brokers – depending on your temperament you'll be more suited to some environments than to others. For many, fund management is a stressful existence and in some firms especially so – there's no point entering an academic hothouse if it's not your thing. A firm's atmosphere depends to a huge extent on the individuals who work there – it doesn't necessarily follow that all hedge funds are run by megalomaniacs and all private-client outfits by kindly old men with a fondness for claret.

Let's now have a look at some of the fund-manager stereotypes you might encounter. Again, it goes without saying that this list is far from exhaustive.

a) Mr Safe Hands

Painstaking, pedantic and thoroughly professional, he does what it says on the tin. A long-only stalwart, he's neither a risk-taker nor a trendsetter, and relaxes on his holidays by reading books on investment. Don't expect much in the way of camaraderie from this one – his regard for himself is matched only by his disdain for frivolity.

b) Mr Up and Coming

Rising hedge-fund star and scourge of a generation, he strives hard to win the respect of his superiors and the dislike of his peers. Not one for social niceties, he's ruthless, rich and getting richer, his ambition as blatant as the chip on his shoulder.

c) Superwoman

In good times an inspiration for women everywhere but in bad a freak of genetics, she's imperiously attractive and a tabloid editor's dream, juggling chief executives, children and charwomen with the skill of a bad-tempered high-wire walker.

d) Mr Know-It-All

He's the best in the business and he knows it. Self-assured, self-obsessed and self-regarding, he can afford to be generous. Even people outside the City have heard of him – he's an all-singing, all-dancing public-relations machine. Investing is an intellectual dogfight he won't and cannot lose – making money from his genius is, quite literally, a bonus.

e) Mr Moribund

He is fluent in Swiss-German and has a home high in the hills above Lake Zurich and a visit to his office is an analyst's nightmare. Cold, ascetic and unforthcoming, he navigates markets with a surgeon's scalpel, snoozing his way through brokers' phone calls and knocking off early most afternoons to tend his garden.

f) Mr Ex-Broker

Canny, pompous and politically astute, he never quite manages to wash away the stain of the sell side. Convinced he deserves a place at high table but fooling no one, he's brutal with brokers and brilliant at passing other people's opinions off as his own.

g) Lord Leisure Time

He excels at accepting other people's invitations, has a golf swing as rhythmic as a Mozart concerto and regards fund management as another would a part-time hobby. Regularly found in private-client departments, he takes the 'Chairman's train'[34] to work and has the most uncontroversial of opinions, although he often has trouble remembering what they were.

h) Mr Inside Job

Machiavellian, reptilian and persistent, he never takes no for an answer. Leading the authorities a merry dance the length and breadth of Europe, he hides out in his tax-free lair and spends all day whispering down the telephone to equally unscrupulous brokers and bankers. Loves hot gossip, brown envelopes and clever accountants – he didn't get this rich by playing straight!

i) Mr Nervous Energy

Disorganised, exasperating and excitable in equal measure, however hard he tries he can't switch off from the job. Driven to distraction by what he's doing wrong and what he imagines everybody else is doing right, his is a restless existence occasionally punctured by shafts of sunshine.

Let's make no mistake about it – managing a fund is a relentless battle against the elements. If you fancy an easy life it's simpler to be a broker. As soon as your name is up in lights others will queue up to shoot it down. For fund managers there's a need for constant accountability, nowhere to hide when you get it wrong and a nagging fear that you don't know what you're doing. Occasionally the genius of a generation appears, someone who does know what he's doing and backs it up with statistics, but most are content to muddle

34 The 'Chairman's train' is a train that runs at a civilised hour of the morning. Unlike chief executives and finance directors, the average chairman doesn't hurry in to work at the crack of dawn. If he comes in at all, he takes breakfast in a first-class carriage, reads the *Daily Telegraph* from cover to cover and steps out on to the platform at Paddington just as the clock is striking ten.

through, rejoicing in their successes and phlegmatic about their failures.

Back in 2003–07 humility was not an attribute too often associated with investors – they were only too happy to shout details of their performance from the rooftops. Pumped up with delusions of grandeur and laden with leverage, most talk was of 'shooting the lights out'. These days, however, they're a little more contrite, feeling their way slowly but surely back into the post-apocalyptic world.

Viva Las Vegas!

As financial markets have become more sophisticated, so the investment community has become more diversified in terms of both how and in what it invests. You only have to leaf through the financial press to see the acres of newsprint dedicated to all the different funds operating around the world today.

Via our savings, most of us are exposed to fund managers. Pension funds, insurance companies, banks, charities, universities, government bodies and individuals the world over all control pools of capital that need to be managed and invested by professionals.

As a fund manager the ability to gauge whether an asset is a good or bad investment is your raison d'être. Although there's a mathematical element to investing, over time you'll realise that intuition and having a sixth sense are just as important. George Soros, one of the world's leading investors, claims that he can anticipate a market crash before most people because his back plays up whenever catastrophe is about to strike.

Investors are professional soothsayers and investing is a game, as much an art as it is a science. A patchwork quilt

of intuition, intellectual process, detective work, calcu-
lation, psychology, speculation and luck, only hindsight
lets you have the answers, but if you play the game then
you've got a good chance of being right more often than
you're wrong.

A good example of this is the dot-com boom of 1999.
Back then the shares of most technology companies went
through the roof, in some cases increasing 40 or even 50
times in a matter of months. Now, this explosion bore no
relation to what was going on in the real world – there
had been no seismic shift in the profitability of these
businesses. What had happened was that technology
stocks had seized investors' imaginations. It was the year
before the millennium and the press was full of stories of
how each and every company would have to hire
consultants to protect them from the 'millennium bug', a
glitch that would bring computer networks to their knees.
In the event, fears of a glitch proved over-cooked and the
world continued as normal, but so exaggerated had been
the hysteria among businesses and so great the optimism
among investors that technology stocks had rocketed.

The other factor was that the internet had begun to
penetrate the public consciousness. Previously a fringe
activity, it was becoming apparent that it could revolutionise
all manner of businesses and industries. In an age before the
arrival of Facebook, price-comparison websites and internet
banking, investors focused on the pioneers of the age –
Yahoo!, eBay and Amazon. The promise of supernormal
growth rates was the talk of the town and investors were on
the prowl for the next big success story. It didn't matter how
coherent or how spurious a business a company had – every
boat rose on the tide of the great internet revolution. Many
of these stocks would never make money (and most never
did), but all commanded stratospheric valuations.

As a consequence, during 1999 and 2000 it was no use fund managers looking for companies with sound business models or reliable profit streams – stocks like Cadbury Schweppes were condemned for their consistency and castigated for their lack of sex appeal. Analysts in 'old economy' sectors like chemicals and tobacco were forced to give presentations arguing that even their staid old stocks were sprinkled with the internet's magic dust. To make money you had to embrace the zeitgeist and climb aboard the technology train, closing your eyes and forsaking all you'd once held most sacred – assets, profits and cash flow.

Bubbles have been occurring since the beginning of time (cf the South Sea Bubble of the early 18th century or the Mid-West gold rush 100 years later), and you should be on your guard when investors, brokers and journalists start heralding the arrival of a brand new 'paradigm'. In the City people are only too ready to believe that things have changed a) for ever and b) for the better. More often than not, however, they confuse paradigm with fallacy.

It's much easier said than done, but the clever investor gets to the party early, makes his money and then gets out before the bubble bursts. Many investors, both professional and private, were left caught short in May 2000 when the market decided that the tech boom was nothing but a fantasy.

It's hard to know how critical to be – how many of us leave a party early if we're having the time of our lives? Asking an investor to jump off the merry-go-round in 2007 was akin to persuading a man to leave a date with the girl of his dreams and go home to bed alone, leaving her to turn her attention to other suitors.

But the winners in 2008 were those who abandoned the girl and went to bed. Others, basking in pools of self-congratulation, were left high and dry when the music stopped. Dismissed and derided as little more than trigger-happy gamblers, they were revealed for the impostors they were. These days speculation as to an investor's performance has been all but replaced by a fascination with his plight – fund managers do *Schadenfreude* as well as anyone.

Stepping Down From Your High Horse

If investing institutional money, a fund manager will have clients too – these are the providers of the capital that you manage. Such people run/work for a variety of organisations – they might be responsible for a company pension scheme, represent a charity, university or family or be a wealthy individual with their own account.

Although most firms have an in-house marketing department to take care of the legwork (such as fielding irritating calls from investors), fund managers also have to play their part. For most the process of marketing can be something of a drag, involving traipsing off to far-flung parts of the country several times a year and having to justify yet another quarter of shoddy performance to an unsympathetic audience. For others, however, the experience can be more pleasurable, especially if you have delivered and/or like the sound of your own voice.

Ultimately a fund manager lives or dies by his performance – in this way it is the City role with the greatest accountability. Nothing sharpens the mind quite like the prospect of a visit to a board of pension-fund trustees when you have blown yet more of their money and are underperforming your peers. The last thing an investor wants is to lose an important mandate – the City is littered with fund managers who suddenly ceased to be relevant.

Other major providers of capital include private banks, sovereign wealth funds, insurance companies (vast organisations that tend to manage their assets in house) and 'funds of funds' (funds that invest their capital in a variety of stand-alone hedge funds). The latter helped fuel the hedge-fund boom, had similarly lavish fee structures and performed as badly as the hedge funds in 2008, despite claiming to offer a far more balanced investment proposition. As a consequence they suffered terribly post the credit crunch as investors pulled the plug, with some estimates putting 2011 assets under management at around 70% of the 2007 peak.

In general, capital providers today are much more circumspect. To gain an investor's trust, approval and ultimately his money, fund managers must go to painstaking lengths to provide evidence of long-term track record. For many this isn't easy – few came through the last few years unscathed. Other capital providers have chosen to abandon equity markets altogether, preferring to shovel their money into less volatile instruments such as cash and fixed income. Although total assets under management continue to rise – in August 2012 the *Financial Times* reported that the global hedge-fund industry alone had enjoyed net inflows of $150bn from the beginning of 2010 – equity ownership is at multi-year lows and the fundraising climate remains one of caution and suspicion. Most fund managers are doing well just to keep hold of the assets they have.

Waking the Dead

If the credit crunch was the financial world's disaster, what of those who now stand on the outside pressing their faces up against the glass?

We have already commented on the City's boundless capacity for reinvention, but it does no harm to reinforce the point. Fund managers are no less resourceful than the brokers, traders and analysts who find their way back to the summit. Every time there's a lull in Trimalchio's banquet the guests take a break, dust themselves down and then reassemble for the next course.

If in 2008/09 a fund manager saw his fund closed down and his belongings bundled into the nearest black bag, it didn't necessarily spell the financial ruin of his family. Over time fund managers have reappeared in a number of different guises:

a) Restart the clock.

The preferred but the most difficult option is to pretend that disaster never actually struck. First they wind up a badly performing fund, returning to investors any capital that remains, and then they create a new fund with a second set of investors.

But why not soldier on with the first fund?

The reason is simple – fees, or to put it more succinctly, performance fees. If a fund works on a two and twenty model and is down 40% in Year 1, the manager won't earn a performance fee until the fund has recovered all of its losses and moves into profit, however long this takes. It's therefore much more lucrative to shut it down, raise fresh capital and start a new fund, thereby closing your eyes to any moral objections. You don't have to move company to do this – it's amazing how many investors have quietly reassumed positions with their old employers.

> SOME FIRMS PREFER to stick with the devil they know. As markets recovered in mid-2009 and hedge funds looked for new recruits, they faced a choice: re-hire someone they'd sacked a year earlier (no doubt for burning through tens of millions of client assets) or take on a new recruit with a cleaner record but less experience. Some re-engaged their old employees, rejecting others on the basis that they had limited experience in managing (and losing) large sums of money. Of course, this tactic often didn't work. Many of those who were re-hired were re-fired in 2010/11, having fallen victim – yet again – to capricious markets.

b) Scurry back under the sell-side rock whence you came.

Some firms, however, despise the devil they know. In 2003–07 the buy side expanded as people flooded over from the other side of the fence. As it contracted, the traffic flow reversed, as fund managers swallowed their pride and trudged back to their alma mater. Although many got their old jobs back, returning is not always a cast-iron certainty, particularly at times of economic weakness.

c) Go back to school.

The short-sighted but idealistic option, people leave the City and quite literally go back to school, becoming economics teachers and expressing their delight at escaping the rat race. How long they stay there, on the other hand, is another matter. It doesn't take a genius to work out that a combination of resurgent City + dwindling bank account + unhappy wife + grass-is-greener syndrome all eventually point to a renewal of the daily commute.

Working Conditions

These days fund managers have it pretty good in terms of working hours, pay and perks.

One of the main attractions of the job is that, like that of a broker or trader, your working day is not project-based but revolves around the hours the market is open. As a consequence most fund managers leave the office not long after the market shuts (indeed most offices will be deserted by 6pm GMT), and you will rarely, if ever, work at weekends or be bothered outside office hours (in stark contrast to your peers in corporate finance).

Many fund managers, particularly those responsible for covering international markets or companies with overseas operations, can expect to be intimately familiar with airports, airline timetables and certain hotels (such as the one in Frankfurt where the adult films are free), but most find that foreign travel a) breaks up the monotony of office life, b) affords the opportunity to visit an exotic array of people and places and c) provides an excuse to behave lamentably at somebody else's expense.

We have already seen how the hedge-fund boom revolutionised buy-side pay structures, with remuneration being linked directly to performance and those in the highest echelon commanding eye-watering salaries, and this has helped move the industry closer to, if not overtake, the sell-side average. In fact, society loves to indulge in Chinese Whispers, with people concocting sensational rumours as to the size of a hedge-fund manager's pay package and then hearing these same rumours repackaged and exaggerated several months later. If you say,

'Have you heard? Ryan earned $20m last year',

you shouldn't be surprised if somebody then approaches you and tells you with breathless excitement,

'I can't believe it! That bastard Ryan earned $50m last year.'

However, the staggering sums of money involved have not prevented many fund managers falling prey to the same frustrations felt by their sell-side peers – unless you're in a position of influence bonuses are discretionary and one person's good performance (and his pay) can be compromised by another's shortcomings. Firms are forever concocting ingenious ways of tying employees in for the long term – tricks include issuing equity in the form of illiquid/untradeable shares or insisting that you roll up a proportion of your earnings back into the fund.

On the other hand, many firms are privately owned and hence are free from much of the interference, both state and media, that has dogged the sell side. There's no need to fret – if you work for a fund that performs, you shouldn't have much to worry about where pay is concerned.

Conclusion

By any standards the last few years have been remarkable. Fund management has careered at a rate of knots from ugly sister to belle of the ball to public enemy number one. Everyone, from City grandee to financial ingénue, has a view on the alchemists from Berkeley Square.

Posterity will look back on the madness of the past few years and ask (with no little justification) why no one saw it coming. But we all remember the reality – most people were too busy admiring their reflections to pay much attention to the canary in the coalmine.

Investors talk about riding bubbles and avoiding their aftermath but most failed to appreciate their pride of place in the biggest bubble of them all – the credit crunch of 2007. They were like the children in the story book who don't spot that the seesaw they're sitting on is in fact a crocodile.

A period of (relative) calm has since descended and that's no bad thing. Bad fund managers are being weeded out from the good and investors are leaving the casino and returning to normal life (or whatever passes as it).

But, like it or not, the goalposts have shifted for ever, and what was once normal is no longer so. As long as performance-related fee structures remain in place, fund management will remain the place to be if you want to get rich. But this time there's a twist – you'll now have to demonstrate you know what you're doing.

— 5 —

CORPORATE FINANCE *OR* INVESTMENT BANKING

*'I count three silk-crepe ties, one Versace silk-satin
woven tie, two silk foulard ties, one silk Kenzo, two silk
jacquard ties. The fragrances of Xeryus and Tuscany and
Armani and Obsession and Polo and Grey Flannel and
even Antaeus mingle, wafting into each other, rising from
the suits and into the air, forming their own mixture:
a cold, sickening perfume.'*

— BRET EASTON ELLIS, *American Psycho*

IN A WORLD of one-upmanship, there's no industry
more hierarchical than corporate finance. If any branch of
the City still personifies the old days, where boys were
boys and men were men, this is it. Performance-based
pay structures and technological innovations may have
altered the buy side and trading landscapes for ever, and
youngsters barely out of school may be strutting their
stuff atop sales desks and hedge funds, but corporate
finance remains the place where experience counts, where
you don't get to be a prefect or smoke with impunity until
you reach maturity.

So much of the City evokes the playground, and corporate
finance is the school where the bigger boys win. You'll
have to accept it for what it is – a rite of passage – if you
want to survive. You suffer today but you'll prosper
tomorrow, that's the deal. Just remember – 20 years ago

the managing director with the grey hair and expensive smile was standing in your little shoes.

In a Nutshell

Corporate financiers (or 'investment bankers') give advice to companies (or 'clients') and help them carry out transactions (or 'deals'). Advice comes in many shapes and sizes (it can be structural, legal or regulatory in nature or specific to a country, industry or type of transaction), and typical transactions include mergers, acquisitions and the raising of capital, both debt and equity. Most fees are payable only on the successful conclusion of a deal – a key difference when one compares corporate finance to other white-collar professions – and explains much of the behaviour and many of the attitudes that we shall come to explore.

Cult Following

It's 9am. You fight your way out of the station, along the street and in through the door of your neo-classical office façade. You pass through the turnstile, get into and out of the lift and swipe your security card on the reader (corporate-finance departments resemble fortresses – Chinese Walls must be maintained).

You open the door, go through it and look around you. Everything's silent. There's nobody there. Is it Christmas?

No, it isn't. It's a normal day in corporate finance. Welcome to the world of all-night endeavour.

Picture the scenario. You share an apartment with a friend. You're both graduates. He works as a broker and you work as an investment banker. He leaves when you're asleep and returns just as your day gets serious. You go in late and go home very late, working nights and most weekends. A month goes by and you never set eyes on each other.

This isn't some far-fetched nightmare; this is reality. Corporate finance is a socially destructive profession. It's a boot camp without the military fatigues, where offices come equipped with sleep pods, toothbrush holders and shirt-vending machines. Firms differ as to the intensity of the workload, but you can be sure of one thing: in most places people compete to see who can stay awake the longest. Investment bankers make research analysts and their obsession with face time look like schoolgirls.

But despite the rumours of austerity, chastity and sleep deprivation, fresh conscripts aren't in short supply. University production lines belch out the brightest and the best and banks crank up the propaganda in an effort to turn their heads (see below). Are you loyal? Yes, sir! Are you devoted? Of course I am, sir! Can you show application? In bucket loads, sir! Do you want a social life? No, I don't, sir! Then sign (away your life) here now. You're the elite and don't you forget it!

More than any other City profession, investment banking has a purity that attracts the zealot. There's something about raw, unbridled capitalism that can brainwash the most hardy of souls. Year in, year out, investment banks serve up the magic potion and graduates fight tooth and nail to drain the glass.

CORPORATE FINANCE IS the only City discipline where the summer intern has a value. Unlike client-facing roles where he can do nothing but a) observe and slowly lull himself to sleep or b) clean out cupboards and file papers (while earning astronomical sums for the privilege), corporate finance internships are a way of getting young do-gooders to do all the tasks full-time employees would rather avoid and save human-resources departments time and effort – there's no need to go through the usual graduate hiring rigmarole (known in the UK as the 'Milk Round'), if the candidates have already proved themselves. Internships are all to do with the survival of the fittest – those who baulk at the workload or grumble at the lack of sleep are hunted down and excommunicated.

Mumbo Jumbo

The 'Milk Round' is a circus of quite mind-boggling proportions, and puts anything that the *Cirque du Soleil* has to offer well into the shade. Every year between December and February caravans of bankers, lawyers, accountants and management consultants make the pilgrimage from London to the country's leading universities. There they a) hold interviews, b) hand out glossy brochures with pictures of healthy, happy bankers (most of whom are actors) and c) launch oceans of alcohol and canapés on to a horde of undergraduates, some of whom ask what they assume to be intelligent questions to bored-looking types with name badges. If you have any sense you'll stand in the corner and say nothing – there's a danger of drinking too much and insulting someone you shouldn't.

At the end of February the circus returns to London where the most almighty scrimmage for jobs takes place. If you get through round one (and rounds two, three and four in some banks), this is the time when you face 'assessment centres' and a barrage of final-round interviews.

Interviewers might not be known for their sympathy, but they're all united by a common creed: they all know you know nothing (even if you haven't worked it out yet). Most young people imagine that they need to demonstrate knowledge of the financial world, and so scour the press for up-to-date information, harangue relatives and raid websites, with the consequence that they have the most bewildering array of material at their fingertips. Most interviewers, however, are unconcerned as to whether you can tell a hedge fund from a hedgerow, and take the logical approach of selecting those they consider to be the least ghastly.

Most interview candidates either a) buckle under the pressure or b) fudge together everything they've ever learned and hurl it back at the questioner. Very few are able to give considered answers, invent responses on the spot or admit it when they don't know something – it's all too easy to memorise replies to every conceivable question.

Stick to what (little) you know and answer the question (if you can). Many graduates fall into the trap of trying to be too clever. If a managing director with the face and bearing of a gravedigger asks,

'So, tell me, what do you think about the market?'

Most will reel off a series of facts they've learned by heart. What you don't then want to hear him remark is,

'Very sage, I must say. Couldn't have put it better myself, although for the record Nicolas Sarkozy is no longer President of France.

TELLING AN INTERVIEWER that you're motivated by money is always a dangerous tactic, especially for a wannabe graduate. While at 32 everyone accepts that money is your major motivation (you wouldn't still be in the industry if it wasn't), at 22 you're assumed to be sufficiently bright-eyed to make (and believe) statements such as,

'I just love markets. I've been following them for years. As a child I invested my pocket money in stocks.'

Or,

'Working on deals must be so thrilling. I can't wait to get involved.'

Graduate training programmes across the City see ice-cold ambition clash head on with juvenile delinquency. Nothing has changed from the nursery school of 20 years earlier – the naughty boys (and girls) sit at the back, shout abuse and roll their eyes while the sober, the virtuous and the deaf clamour for the teacher's approval at the front.

In firms where roles have already been pre-ordained, many graduates will take only a passing interest in the economic and financial theory being shovelled their way, preferring instead to see who can fall foulest of the expensively employed teacher (driving him or her to resignation is the ultimate goal – nothing angers authority more than incessant chatter) or who can end up in bed with whom (for graduate training programmes think fresher's week with $75,000 salaries). Some will even daub textbooks and blackboards with obscene graffiti, safe in the knowledge that the teacher will be too surprised and/or embarrassed to take any action.

Other firms keep their powder dry and their graduates guessing, suspecting (correctly) that a sense of insecurity leads to better behaviour. You should expect to spend month upon month watching (enthralled or in horror – it's your call) as prospective brokers, traders and bankers stampede to demonstrate the extent of their knowledge. Even after securing a permanent place many graduates are still loath to admit themselves at a loss. Banks like nothing better than to herd the little prigs into a room and take them down a peg or seven.

'Can anyone tell me why so many hedge funds ran into trouble post the credit crunch?'

Up go the hands.

'You, the girl with the blond hair. . .'

'A hedge fund is an unregulated pool of capital that seeks absolute rather than relative. . .'

'That's the dictionary definition, not the answer to my question. You, the guy at the back with the ridiculous braces. . .'

'There was no proper risk assessment. The VARs weren't being properly controlled.'

'Even if it's true, what does that actually mean? Do you have any idea?'

Or,

'Why do banks underwrite? You, the gentleman at the front. . .'

'Underwriting is all about the spreading of risk.'

'Is it really? How's that then?'

'If a deal goes sour the client can fall back on the bank.'

'But that's not what I asked you. We do it because it earns us a fee.'

Ask a graduate what his job entails and you'll receive a variety of answers. If he works in sales, trading or research he's likely to have cottoned on quite quickly to what he's supposed to be doing, but even after several months in the job, aspirant investment bankers can still seem confused and will hide behind all manner of tongue-twisting terminology. MBA graduates appear enlightened by comparison.

'Yeah, well, we're helping a client with a de-leveraged de-merger, but I can't talk about it because it's top secret.'

Cue blank faces and embarrassed laughter, especially if the poor fellow's on a date.

But there's no shame in being confused – corporate finance isn't meant to be simple. If it was, experience would count for naught and 25-year-olds would mastermind billion-dollar deals.

§

SUCKING UP TO the right people (or those you perceive to be) doesn't necessarily guarantee you the pick of the jobs on offer. Much of the graduate training programme will involve stints with the different departments of your firm, and how you behave when addressing envelopes or carrying boxes for underlings in the Compliance department can matter as much as how dutifully you sit by the side of the head of trading, no more useful (in a commercial sense) than a summer intern. People's perception of you counts for so much more than the reality – what you want potential bosses to believe is that you're a desirable commodity. If you'd like to work in corporate finance, you may not choose to proposition the Head of Corporate Finance directly. Instead you might decide to spread rumours of your widespread desirability, so much so that he eventually asks his counterpart in human resources,

'What's this I've been hearing about young Fortescue? Apparently everyone wants to take him on. I think I'd better have lunch with him.'

The Head of Human Resources is always a vital ally. One graduate made the fatal mistake of muddling him up with a friend of the same surname, sending an email that read,

'Hurry up, you gimp. We've got to leave in five minutes.'

This prompted the magisterial reply,

'Never in the history of this firm has the Head of Human Resources been called a "gimp" by a graduate trainee.'

The graduate buried his head in his hands. Coincidence or not, six months later he was out of the door. Apparently the firm had 'no further need of his services'.

A Broad Church

Investment banking comprises a multitude of activities. Different banks do slightly different things, but for the sake of simplicity we'll split everything into two camps: 'advisory' and 'financing'. As an employee of one, however, you should expect similar responsibilities to, and regular contact with, colleagues of the other – all too often investment-banking activities tread on each other's toes (and bonus pots).

Advisory, which in most firms includes the functions of mergers and acquisitions (or M&A) and corporate broking, consists of a) the strategic and tactical advice that investment banks give to clients such as companies, families and government entities and b) the ability to help effect a transaction (from a structural, technical and mechanical perspective). Financing, on the other hand, involves the raising of capital (both equity and debt) for these and other clients, often in connection with transactions where the firm is playing an advisory role.

CORPORATE BROKERS EXIST only in the UK and are essentially a company's eyes and ears around the market, relating any investor desires or anxieties and funnelling information back and forth between a business and its shareholders. Depending on its size/sense of self-importance, a company will give official mandates to one or two corporate brokers. Although as a general rule (but not exclusively) M&A advisers concentrate on big-picture strategy and corporate brokers on market-facing issues (such as equity issuance, drafting results announcements, helping company executives buy or sell stock and organising investor road shows), in many firms the two are inter-related, with both providing help and advice on a variety of subjects. Indeed it's quite usual for close corporate broking contacts to result in lucrative M&A transactions.

Old is Beautiful

Investment banking and the progression of capitalism are one and the same. In a world in which the strong subsume the weak, the rich get richer and 'biggest is best' cuts the smartest cloth, bankers and company executives/ megalomaniacs can be each other's greatest allies.

Rainmakers, kingmakers or dealmakers, call them what you will, senior bankers are under constant pressure to deliver. Like the snooker player who thinks two shots ahead or the DJ who spins three records at once, they're forever scheming, manipulating and manoeuvring, thirsting for fees as they run from client to client. In an industry where league tables can be sliced, diced and re-sliced to suit every bank's purposes, bankers are assessed and re-assessed on a constant basis. You're only as good as your last deal. And revenues are just one side of the story – market share matters too. Bagging a $3m fee means nothing if the guy down the street/in the office next door brings home ten times that amount.

The successful banker is a jack-of-all-trades. Adviser, salesman, counsellor and sounding board to name but several, he must combine reason with resilience and temper gluttony with self-restraint. Giving bad advice and/or conning a client into the wrong deal might not stand him in good stead for the long term, but for many the prospect of bagging a fee and moving on is all too tempting. In due course we'll have a look at the ways in which bankers pass the buck.

Patience is a senior banker's greatest virtue. Transactions earn fees but advice costs nothing. You can spend years helping a client navigate the most shark-infested of waters and still not receive a penny in fees. A client might choose to sit on his hands or, as is more likely, deals that you thought were nailed-on certainties will suddenly unravel/lead to a dead end (a rough estimate is that nine in ten 'buy-side'[35] deals go nowhere). On the other hand, you can't afford to rest on your laurels – if you do you'll soon be superseded. While in some countries (such as the UK) companies employ official advisers,[36] in theory anyone can

---

35 In investment banking parlance 'buy side' = representing the potential acquirer of an asset. This is not to be confused with the other City 'buy side', ie the fund-management community.

36 In addition to the corporate brokers mentioned in the previous note, UK companies also have official M&A advisers. Companies aren't obliged to use these advisers for every transaction, but more often than not will involve them in some kind of capacity, especially when defending themselves from hostile suitors.

pitch an idea and win an investment-banking mandate. Even though this is an industry where relationships are all-important, it's not uncommon for one adviser to be elbowed out of the way by another.

This can happen for any number of reasons. People fall out, management moves on, somebody turns up with a better idea or a company grows too big for its boots, dazzled by the bright lights and yearning for the (not necessarily) superior services of a larger bank. In this last instance the cuckolded adviser can do nothing – kicking up a fuss will only damage the relationship – and so settles unhappily for a minor role in a ménage à trois.

Transactions come in many shapes and sizes – eg A is buying B, C is selling D, E is trying to protect itself from F, G wants to raise capital and H wants to restructure its debt. It's worth making the point now: no one deal is the same, but it sure helps to have experience. What you learn in the past will guide you in the future, and the more you've learned the wiser you should be.

Companies don't (normally) hire banks because they have the most palatial offices, the most alluring secretaries or the most industrious graduates. They hire those that a) give the best advice and b) get the job done. And while there are occasions when banks appear on the team sheet because of who they are and not because of what they offer, most of the time individuals clinch deals, not institutions.

Company executives don't think,

'Let's get Morgan Stanley as our lead adviser. We don't know their main men Smith and Jones, but I'm sure it will all work out.'

Instead they think,

'Let's get our friends Smith and Jones to be the leads. Are they still at Morgan Stanley or have they moved on?'

Only once they've secured the services of those they trust might they also add,

'We've got Smith and Jones to be our leads, but I think it also makes sense to have Goldman on board. We don't expect them to do much, but having them there will make us look better.'

In this industry long-term relationships are critical. The old school tie confers everything and clients tend to value continuity over the claims of a Johnny-come-lately. In a world where anyone can approach anyone, you can spend months hammering on a company's door with the most brilliant of ideas, but if you don't know the management or the board and they don't know you, you can forget about securing a mandate. Only if you work for a firm that can bring something specific to the party (such as sector expertise or political contacts[37]), might you walk through a door that would otherwise remain barred.

BANKERS AND BLUFFING go hand in hand – they can sometimes make brokers look profound! You have only to sit in a meeting and watch your boss skate over the thinnest of ice, telling the most appalling lies about a) your firm and b) his prowess and regurgitating every fact he's

37 Bankers and politicians fall over themselves to do each other's bidding. If the US Treasury Department is an annexe of Wall Street, politicians assist bankers by a) opening doors and b) smoothing over any issues that might otherwise hinder a deal (eg it was rumoured that the Lloyds/HBOS tie-up in 2008 would never have been sanctioned without the personal intervention of Gordon Brown). Politicians on the boards of leading banks have included Tony Blair at JP Morgan and John Major at Credit Suisse.

> ever learned about a given subject. As with brokers,
> bluffing gets easier the more respected you become.
> People are more likely to believe what you say.

Compared with most other City professions investment banking is a gruelling existence, a promise of long-term gain for a pound of flesh today and another tomorrow. M&A in particular is a marathon not a sprint, with never-ending hours for juniors, no rapid promotions and only a gradual increase in responsibility. If you seek instant gratification then forget it – this isn't for you.

Let's now have a look at the individuals in the investment banking food chain:

Managing Director

In corporate finance people talk about the importance of 'grey hair'. This is not a sartorial preference but a confirmation of the value placed on experience. Banks don't let young Turks take charge of mega-deals – a CEO and his chairman want to appoint men who've seen years of active service, who've been round the block and back. In most firms you won't reach managing director (MD) level until you have completed between 10 and 15 years of service.[38]

The brains behind any transaction, the MD has the credibility and the contacts to make deals happen, but the buck stops with him if they don't. He wields the power of life and death over his subordinates. Forget anniversaries,

---

38 Bankers never seem to have a problem finding employment once they leave the City. There's great demand for their services from both industry and governmental bodies. This yet again highlights the value of the old school tie – no matter how bad a banker's advice there's always a home for him somewhere!

honeymoons and birthday parties – if a deal's live he'll track you down wherever you're hiding.

Although his life is preferable to that of a junior (he doesn't have to be in the office late into the night checking documents or changing/running financial models), a managing director can never escape a client's clutches, even when away on vacation. No banker, however influential he might be, likes to admit that he's on holiday. He'll dispel important tactical advice wherever he happens to be – in bed, by the pool or on the beach with seagulls calling in the background and waves lapping at his feet. While colleagues listen in and cringe, by his side stands a glowering wife who had imagined that the years of interrupted holidays and/or dinners would soon be at an end. The onset of technology has only made things worse – bankers check their Blackberries with a regularity that borders on the obsessive, so paranoid are they that they'll miss some vital detail or be left out of the loop.

Managing directors have a variety of skill sets – some are showmen, big-picture thinkers and innovators, while others are technicians, versed in legal, regulatory, tax or sector-specific detail. Depending on their size and/or complexity, different transactions require different numbers of senior bankers, although when times are tough people aren't averse to muscling their way into deals they would normally consider beneath them. As the recent downturn kicked in, work dried up and bankers did their utmost to involve themselves in deals that had little or nothing to do with them. Small clients were surprised and more than a little suspicious to arrive at meetings and find there all manner of senior people they didn't know – just what was this all going to cost?

Director/Vice President

Call him what you will – nexus point, co-ordinator or quarterback – there's much resting on his broad shoulders. More than the other City professions, investment banking is a team game, with seniors and juniors bringing various skills to bear. Managing directors will be charging from country to country and from client to client, and need someone they can rely on to pull everything and everyone together both in the office or behind them on the plane.

In some cases directors/vice presidents will have client responsibilities of their own, although these will be lower down the corporate ladder or related to smaller, less eye-catching deals. Much of their time will be spent beating junior bankers into shape as they collate and collect the material their bosses require.

Working hours might become less arduous as you rise up through the hierarchy, but this is not an industry where you can ever take it easy. If managing directors are under constant pressure to justify their worth and juniors are deemed no more deserving of respite than a serf on a Russian farm, directors and vice presidents will sit brooding in glass offices surveying their terrain like bad-tempered amphibians, dreaming of the day they receive the keys to the magic kingdom.

Some directors or VPs are frighteningly young, although to look at them you wouldn't know it. Skin that does not see sunlight soon takes on a pallid shade of grey, and eyes and cheekbones recede ever further into flesh. Physical imperfections, however, do not prohibit romantic entanglements – the proportion of bankers who get involved with a colleague is staggeringly high. Juniors will be reduced to tears one minute and marrying their tormentors the next, and wives will be heard to tell their husbands (and vice versa – it does happen),

'You were a cruel bastard back then. Whatever did I see in you?'

It's perhaps not surprising when one stops to think about it. Many bankers live such cocooned existences that they struggle a) to meet people outside the office and b) to communicate with those they do.

There's a physical intensity about corporate finance that other City disciplines lack. Deals can take an eternity, and you'll get used to sharing taxis, meeting rooms and dining tables with the same people – both clients and colleagues – for months on end. Stories abound of smouldering glances, frustrated passions and inappropriate behaviour. A client with his hand up your skirt is still a client – in some firms he keeps it there or you leave, it's as brutal as that.

IN 2011 THE BBC commissioned a survey and discovered – lo and behold – that the sexual temperature in the City of London had never risen so high. Never mind the role they had played in wrecking the world economy, modern bankers were more adulterous than their 1980s or 1990s counterparts had ever dreamed of being. Various 'experts' were called on to explain the phenomenon, most of whom concluded that bankers felt emasculated by the collapse in their earning power and so sought solace in the arms of another. Plausible or otherwise – and it does seem questionable – we cannot deny that the huge increase in the numbers of female City workers has quickened the sexual pulse. Today's financial world is hardly the equal opportunities utopia most investment banks would have you believe, but it's a far cry from the all-male bastion of thirty years ago.

Associate/Analyst

This might be the dog end of the job, a life of never-ending enslavement and exhaustion, but analysts take an almost fanatical pride in their nocturnal endeavours. Whiling away night after night preparing pitches or inputting meaningless data into meaningless spreadsheets might not be your idea of fun, but think again. Hard graft can become addictive – this is a world where people compete to stay up all night or see how much holiday they can roll over to next year.

As in equity research, numbers a) form the basis of most arguments and b) can be manipulated to suit a banker's purposes. If he wants Company A to take over Company B then he needs to be able to demonstrate the merits of the deal (such as the improved positioning, the boost to profits and the cost savings/synergies the combined entity would enjoy). But his job is to charm the clients, not fudge the numbers. And that's where the analyst comes in.

As soon as you begin your employment you will be drilled and re-drilled, taught how to analyse company accounts, build financial models and profile different businesses. You gather and package the raw data that others check, re-check, refine and pass on up the chain. You can't take any short cuts – your superiors won't let you – and you'll battle on through the night, screaming blue murder until, like the most creative of accountants, you finally force the squarest of pegs into the roundest of holes.

It's not surprising that attrition rates among new graduates are through the roof. The early years are, more than anything else, a test of stamina. Banks take a similar approach to the military – they flog you to death and see how much pain you can take. There's something psychotic about an existence where you sit around doing nothing for most of the day and then, as the sun is setting and your boss is walking out of the door, come the fateful words,

'Have this on my desk by nine o'clock tomorrow morning.'

Even though you're expecting them, they never fail to grate. Just once, you pray, just once, I might get away early tonight.[39] So you labour on into the night, trudge home in the early hours and collapse into bed. The next day you sleepwalk to the office and hand in your home-work at the appointed hour.

And then you wait. Nothing happens. So you wait some more. It's now 11 o'clock and no one's asked to see you. Only at midday does your boss acknowledge receipt of your work, and even then he doesn't give it another glance. Aren't you wondering why you bothered?

Even worse are the words,

'I need this for Sunday evening,'

when it's Friday afternoon and you're staring into the abyss of your weekend.

'But it's my mother's birthday and my family have flown in especially from Australia.'

Or,

'But I haven't had a day off all year and I'm going on holiday tomorrow!'

Tough – no one cares. You'll do what they say, whether you're skiing, saving the sick or hobnobbing with royalty.

39 Getting home early on a weekday is such a luxury that most analysts won't know what to do with themselves. They'll have nothing in the diary – there's no point arranging anything if you always have to cancel it. On the rare occasions that you do venture out you'll be no fun anyway, boring your friends with corporate chitchat and falling asleep at the table!

The job does have its perks, even though everything's relative. You don't have to a) pay for dinner at your desk or b) struggle home on public transport after an 18-hour shift. You can expense food and taxis if you're in the office after a certain hour (9pm in most banks). Some analysts will remain at work for no other reason than to milk the system, stopping their taxi off en route to buy raw meat that they'll cook at home and expense to the firm!

§

> IN ANOTHER MILITARY parallel, some firms are so sophisticated that you can order food direct to your desk via the company intranet. Rather than call the local curry house or pizza delivery boy, you can have a chicken korma or a pepperoni with mushrooms brought straight to your desk with two clicks of the mouse!

You'll take enormous pride in seeing a deal you've spent months slaving over adorn the front page of a national newspaper. Friends and family, however, won't always share your excitement. They'll only pretend to know what you're talking about and will be quietly appalled that you're wasting your youth on something quite so vapid.

On rare occasions you'll get to perform in front of clients. Junior bankers presenting a page of a pitch for the first time are a sight to behold. You'll be told the night before what you'll be presenting, and you'll spend the next 12 hours in a state of terror, copying down longhand what you plan to say and rehearsing it over and over again. Most people find their boss more frightening than a client. After all, he's the one who really counts.

When you come to speak, your heart will be racing and your face will be burning. You'll either read your piece verbatim, with everyone around the table (including the client) listening patiently and politely until you gasp for breath, or you'll begin just as your boss is turning over the page, tapping his watch and warning, 'we need to hurry up'. Much of the time you won't even get to speak – juniors are always given the unimportant pages near the back of the book.

After two or three years an analyst becomes an associate – it's a bit like graduating from boot boy to footman in a 19th-century household. Not much changes. The hours are still terrible, but the pay improves and the work becomes that little bit more interesting.

In a case of poacher turned gamekeeper, you now get to supervise the analysts. Be aware, though, that power can go to people's heads and that it's all too easy to turn on people who were once your allies. Bankers can be ruthless, and young bankers especially so – it's the school playground dynamic all over again.

WHERE INVESTMENT BANKING is concerned, there's no such thing as chivalry. Rainmakers will stride off to meetings with a raft of subordinates in tow, paying no attention to the young woman struggling 20 yards behind them underneath a pile of presentations.

Secretary

A Cerberus at the corporate gate, bankers alienate her at their peril. She wields power far above her actual station, controlling diaries, processing expenses and telling white lies where necessary (more often than not 'he's in a meeting at the moment' means 'he's having a lie-in/doing the crossword' or 'he hasn't finished it yet and doesn't dare tell you').

Many secretaries enjoy unparalleled access to their boss's private lives, booking holidays, sending flowers, arranging dinners, and, in extreme cases, siphoning money from their bank accounts (cf the Goldman Sachs assistant who was convicted of stealing $6m from three colleagues). She's also a go-between for many married couples – how many wives call their husbands and slam down the phone on hearing her dulcet tones for the umpteenth time that day?

> SOME SECRETARIES MIGHT go out of their way to 'bag a banker' but be warned: you should avoid sleeping with yours unless your intentions are honourable. You'll generally get into less trouble if you sleep with somebody else's.

Passing the Buck

Alan Greenspan, former Chairman of the US Federal Reserve, was spot on when he coined the term 'irrational exuberance'. Bubbles are dangerous and no more so than in M&A. As markets spiral out of control and the lights flash red, bankers and their clients just can't say no.

To what extent M&A benefits the investor or adds value is a moot point. If in some eyes it is an extension of Western values, a harnessing of capitalism's animal spirit, in others it is a travesty, a way in which bankers, lawyers and management teams justify their existences at the expense of the shareholder. While some companies enter into shrewd, timely acquisitions that improve their standing, others are deal-making junkies, renowned for delighting their bankers but infuriating their shareholders.

The peak of every cycle is characterised by hubris, by deals that enrich bankers but bring down empires, and the last two decades have featured some of the most egregious. While you'll struggle to find anyone today who'll defend AOL's move for Time Warner or Royal Bank of Scotland's acquisition of ABN Amro, back then they were lauded as ground-breaking examples of corporate foresight. Pity the RBS employees who lost their jobs as a result of 'internal reorganisation'.

For a captain of industry, the career-defining deal is always the most dangerous. Business is booming, markets are soaring and shareholders are eating out of his hands. So what does he do? He decides to go out in a blaze of glory and leave a legacy.

But legacies can tarnish, and just as a man can forsake his wife of 20 years and then regret it, so an executive can pay over the odds for an asset he doesn't need. Individuals who believe their hype can soon find themselves being picked to pieces by the vultures.

Transactions don't disappoint just because a company pays the wrong price. Much of the rationale behind a deal is based on theory – if we combine A and B then we'll knock this much off our cost base or we'll sell C because we can survive quite comfortably without it. Bankers and management teams are famed for promising things that never materialise, either because they were unrealistic in the first place or because management fails to deliver. Whatever its size, 'execution risk' poses the greatest threat to every infant business.

Timing is also an issue. In a world where investors demand ever more instant gratification, bankers and companies will argue (often with justification) that people all too rarely look to the long term. New companies take time to coalesce – cultures, ground rules and working relationships all need to be established – and few deals take place without there being teething problems. People don't like change; it's as simple as that.

But while a deal is being constructed and then flashed across the globe, this is often forgotten. There's a sex appeal about cross-border, billion-dollar M&A that can appease the most doughty of cynics. The clever banker sells theory, packages probability and learns how to pass the buck. If the deal then blows up in the company's face it's their fault, not his. He may have given them the keys to the car, but they got drunk and drove it off the road.

$

COMPANY EXECUTIVES ARE, of course, quite capable of wrecking the best-laid plans without any help from bankers. Many a deal turns sour or doesn't happen because people can't agree on certain terms or on who will take which role in a newly formed entity. All too often egotism gets in the way of common sense.

Moving with the Times

Empire building is, of course, not a new phenomenon. For centuries people have been looking for ways to line their pockets. In today's world investment banks might be orchestrating the process, but to hold them solely accountable for deals that don't deliver would be doing them a disservice. Company executives and their share-holders belong alongside them in the dock.

Corporate financiers must keep up to date if they want to get paid. To put it another way, they must be chameleons. If 2005–2007 was all about keeping hedge funds happy and loading companies up with cheap debt, banks have sung a very different tune since (and will doubtless be singing a new one tomorrow). An investment banker who told a client back in 2005,

'You're far too conservative. Your business can support twice as much debt. Let us help you fix it up. The market will love you for it',

gave the client different advice in 2008:

'You need to raise money. You've got far too much debt. Let us help you fix it up. The market will love you for it',

and changed his mind again in 2012:

'I know you're worried about over-stretching yourself but, trust me, your cash is only rotting away in the bank. You can't sit on your hands for ever.'

If for nothing else, you have to admire bankers for their nerve. As the fallout from the credit crunch lengthened, however, most of them began to get desperate. Deals were thin on the ground and many transactions taking an eternity to complete as shareholders quibbled over the fine print and found any excuse to delay proceedings. As one banker put it:

'These days it's three times as difficult to earn a dollar of revenue as it used to be.'

Pre the credit crunch, the hedge-fund rationale had run as follows: if a company could borrow more money then it should do so, as long as the return on capital was higher than the cost. In other words, if the new debt cost 5% per annum to service but the return was 6% then the scheme would be considered profit enhancing or 'earnings accretive'. In fact credit was so cheap in those days that from a financial perspective most schemes made sense (until they unravelled). Many companies were encouraged to borrow money and hand it back to shareholders by way of a 'special dividend'.

But in the post-crunch world hedge funds played a different game. As the clouds began to lift and bankers queued up to raise money for companies in distress (of which there were many), the canny investor went on a buying spree, betting that expectations of and subsequent confirmation of a company's solvency would drive its share prices higher. Some stocks rocketed 10 or 20 times as banks performed 'rescue rights issues' (and pocketed enormous fees) and long-suffering shareholders came to the rescue. The latter had no other choice – if they hadn't got involved their investments would have been worthless.

All this serves to highlight that a) bankers can be fickle; b) company executives can be credulous; c) corporate financiers and short-term investors work in tandem; and d) long-term shareholders can be lazy. Hedge funds can be criticised for many things but at least they get their hands dirty. The indolence of many of the long-only fraternity, by contrast, plays straight into the hands of greedy bankers and even greedier management teams. As we saw in the last chapter, abstention is all too often the extent of the shareholder's ire. If they made a stand against some of the more kamikaze corporate adventures then many accidents wouldn't happen.

$

IN RECENT YEARS some investors have tried to buck the trend and make a stand (see *Fund Management*), but we shouldn't hold our breath – history suggests a return to passive acceptance as and when economic conditions stabilise. There's nothing like a bull market to put a shareholder's mind at rest.

The private equity boom of the last few years was part and parcel of the same credit gravy train. If hedge funds were a broker's new best friends then private equity – investment funds that manage portfolios of private (unlisted) companies – was the investment banking equivalent. Like its hedge-fund cousin the industry has been around for decades, but money poured in post the millennium as economies soared and investors began to realise that excellent returns could be made from private as well as from public companies. Buying a stake in a private company confers several advantages – not only is there no share price (and hence no share price volatility/public scrutiny), but investors can also structure the deal in such a way that they control the business without a) committing too much equity and b) taking too much risk.

For investment bankers the rise of the industry was a godsend – gone were the days of hauling themselves over the coals in an attempt to get staid Company A to make a move for conservative Company B. Private equity firms staffed by investment-banking alumni proliferated like mice, were flush with cash and were falling over themselves (and each other) in order to spend it. If a banker had a company to sell all he had to do was flip through his address book and call one of his many friends/former colleagues now working on the other side of the fence. Such was the stampede to do deals that assets were sold at auction to the highest bidder and prices driven to eye-watering and ultimately calamitous levels. Like hedge funds most private equity firms operated two-and-twenty charging structures and – crucially – the capital they managed had to be deployed in order to earn these fees. It was no use it just sitting in the bank earning interest.

And so while some firms bought good businesses and set out to nurture them, many others practised a

leveraged buy-out[40] model that was brutal in its
simplicity: borrow money (sometimes as much as ninety
per cent of the necessary capital), acquire an asset
(which didn't have to be unlisted – public companies
could also be purchased and then delisted), improve it
and flog/'exit' it for a profit, either by selling it to
another buyer (such as a private equity rival) or by
listing/re-listing it on the market for an inflated value.
In many ways it was no different to the way asset-
strippers behaved in the 70s and 80s or to how people
have played the residential housing game. You buy an
asset for 100 with 10 of equity and 90 of debt (that is,
somebody else's money). You then spend two years
improving it, borrowing an extra 10 to do so. During
this period underlying asset prices rise 30%, with banks
prepared to lend an ever-increasing multiple of your
income (salary in an individual's case and profits in a
company's). At the end of the two years you sell your
asset for 140 (ie market growth plus an improvement
premium), pay back the debt of 100 (plus any accrued
interest) and, lo and behold, you have quadrupled your
money.

For many private equity firms the payback was
immediate, especially at the start of the decade when the
market place was less crowded and the deal terms more
favourable. With the help of their investment-banking
cronies they could swoop down upon unsuspecting
companies in the morning and hold the keys to the place
by nightfall. All too often, 'improvement' meant penny-
pinching – selling assets and sacking staff – and much of
the time the new owners sat back and did nothing,
watching on as economies boomed, stock markets

40 A leveraged buy-out is a way of acquiring an asset with somebody else's
money. In 2005 Manchester United was bought by scraping together
(very expensive) debt from a whole variety of sources, including both banks and
hedge funds.

roared and their new trinkets spiked in value. As the boom approached its zenith some firms were no more than asset traders, using their contacts to acquire companies that they shifted on without ever stepping over the threshold.

Now leveraged buy-outs (or 'LBOs') were not a new phenomenon (cf KKR's US$25bn acquisition of RJR Nabisco in 1988, at the time the largest corporate takeover in US history), but this was a world awash with credit and private equity firms took full advantage. As banks and other entities queued up to lend them the money, hedge funds joined the frenzy, setting up private-equity divisions of their own and speculating in stocks they thought would be bid for. In the zany days of 2007 most listed businesses attracted bid rumours, spurious or otherwise.[41] No investor dared short a stock for fear it might be taken over, and bankers, hedge funds and private-equity firms teamed up to buy assets, lend money, inflate prices and pass each other valuable information. By the time the sovereign-wealth funds and their vats of capital were added to the mix the bonfire was well and truly ablaze.

The LBO model, however, has three flaws: it really works only when a) economies are thriving, b) asset prices are rising and c) debt is cheap and readily available. As the credit crunch began to bite, private equity firms foundered in the same quicksand as the hedge funds. When the banks turned off the lending tap both were forced back to basics, hedge funds to make money from the markets and private equity to make inefficient businesses more efficient, both without the benefit of leverage.

---

41 Back then everything and anything was a target. Investors, analysts and bankers dreamt up all manner of crazy schemes. Even GlaxoSmithKline, one of the UK's largest companies, was said to be a target, despite the fact that a potential acquirer would have needed to borrow some $160bn (a sum equal to the UK Department of Health's entire budget for 2012–2013) to finance the deal!

The problem was that many people didn't know how to do this. They simply had no experience.

The private equity industry is a case study in itself, but the fallout from the credit crunch has been, and may well continue to be, long and torrid. Across the world private equity funds still have plenty of money to spend – close to $1tr according to recent estimates – but restrictions on leverage, market volatility and the corresponding dearth of corporate activity have placed many on life support. Having capital is wonderful if you can spend it; if you can't you don't earn fees and your investors (or 'limited partners') will wonder why they gave it to you in the first place. Furthermore exits have been difficult to achieve – nothing gives a fund manager more pleasure than sabotaging the IPO hopes of a private-equity-owned business – and performance has been patchy – many deals done at pre-2008 prices haven't delivered and have required doses of hands-on surgery and/or extra capital. As a consequence many funds have had to revise fee expectations or struggled to raise new capital and been forced to close or limp along like zombies. By way of example, the industry raised globally $683bn of new funds in 2008, whereas it managed only $327bn in 2012. Despite the efforts the industry has made in recent years to re-brand itself as a philanthropic provider of capital, until markets stabilise and leverage returns the pain looks set to continue.

None of this is any consolation to individual companies, many of which are innocent victims of the credit crunch. Whatever the financial climate the wheels of capitalism must keep on turning, and most companies, especially those in the unlisted space, have found capital all but impossible to come by in recent years. While we might vilify banks, hedge funds and private-equity firms for their excesses, we must also remember that they provide solutions to companies in need of funding and hence their retrenchment is cause for concern. But the financial crisis has not only hampered institutional investors. Many businesses, especially those in start-up mode, look to source capital from 'friends and family', but even this has slowed to a trickle as the squeeze on private individuals and their incomes has taken hold.

There may, however, be rays of sunshine amid the gloom. It's still early days, but new providers of capital are emerging from the ruins of the post-credit-crunch landscape. Pension funds and insurance companies are entering the banking sector and making loans directly to borrowers, while alternative investment vehicles such as family offices are taking stakes in public and private companies.

A growing number of wealthy families now run their affairs in the manner of mini-institutions. Before the credit crunch these families entrusted much of their wealth to professional investors such as hedge funds and private-equity firms, but high fees and poor performance led to many families pulling out their capital. Instead some began to invest in companies without the need for a middle man, a process known as 'direct investment'. This trend looks set to continue as more and more families realise that it makes better economic sense to hire a team of investment professionals and do the job themselves rather than pay two and twenty for third-party funds that fail to perform. For companies seeking capital this can only be good news. Family office investors may not be as time efficient as their institutional counterparts, but what they lack in speed they make up for in flexibility. It's their own money so they can spend it how they choose.

One Big Happy Family

From the banker's perspective if not the client's, investment-banking fees are suitably generous. The City takes the view that a) if a client wants good advice then he can afford to pay for it, b) undercutting the competition on fees is in nobody's interest and c) the rewards must offset the risks (many mandates are success-based – if a deal doesn't go through then banks, unlike law firms, don't get paid a penny). Ultimately, that's why bankers earn more than lawyers.

Where advisory roles are concerned, fee pots differ as to the size of the deal, although a small deal can involve just as much work as a large one and can be just as complicated. Rather than take home a pre-specified percentage of the total transaction value (as banks do when raising capital, such as for IPOs or rights issues[42], advisory fees reflect a bank's economic necessities, with most firms starting the clock at around US$3–5m (on the assumption that a minimum of three people will devote a minimum of six months to a transaction).

Mega-deals mean mega-fees, and it is rare for companies to have just one adviser. The largest transactions involve serious manpower (50 bankers and 50 lawyers were said to have worked on keeping Rio Tinto out of BHP's clutches in 2008) and serious money. In its landmark acquisition of Mannesmann, the German conglomerate, in 2000, Vodafone paid out £83bn for the company and

---

42 Companies carry out 'rights issues' when they are seeking to tap the market for capital. In a rights issue a shareholder has the pre-emptive right to buy shares at a discount to the current stock price. If he elects to 'take up his rights' then his percentage holding in the company will be no different from what it was before the process started. Depending on a company's financial health, the discount can be slight or severe. It all comes down to how badly the company needs the money.

£400m in fees, the majority of which went to its banking and legal advisers.

When a company employs a number of advisers they form what is called a 'syndicate'. Banks and individuals can be invited into syndicates for any number of reasons: they might be long-standing, trusted allies of the company's management or board, they might have expertise/clout in a specific area (such as a country or an industry), they might be needed as window-dressing (having an extra luminary in tow never does any harm, even if that luminary offers next to nothing) or they might simply be an old friend of the management. Boutique firms will often gatecrash the most prestigious of parties because a chief executive happens to have gone to school with a managing director.

Syndicates are hierarchical and advisers aren't always equals. In most cases a 'lead' bank or banks will do the bulk of the work and earn the bulk of the fees (which in most cases will be pre-agreed). Some advisers do no more than get engagement letters signed, then sit back and enjoy reading about their exploits in the press.

§

A FEE DISCUSSION is nearly always the final piece of the jigsaw before a deal goes live and agreeing fees that suit each and every party is rarely if ever straightforward. A banker can spend months if not years courting a company and then have to tread a fine line between securing adequate remuneration and not frightening off/irking the client with his excessive demands. The picture is then further complicated by the other snouts in the syndicate trough, all of whom regard their services to be worth more than the lead bank believes. Ultimately a fee agreement is a function of a) what the client can afford to pay and b) what the syndicate members consider to be the economic minimum for their services. Rarely is it the product of what the different parties believe to be 'fair', the goal of most business school negotiating manuals. In finance appealing to somebody's better nature is all too often a waste of time.

Where your firm ranks in a syndicate and how this is presented matters enormously to some bankers. In an M&A transaction the names of all the syndicate members will be printed on the front of the 'offer document' or on a 'tombstone' in a national newspaper advertisement, and where your name sits in relation to those of your peers can cause all manner of controversy. If, for example, your firm is co-lead on a deal, you ideally want your firm's name to appear on the top left of the page (just as a film star will want his or her name to appear first on a poster). If for whatever reason it doesn't, then you might insist that the name appears in a different font size or be raised up above that of your rival.[43]

Like so many other City squabbles, it's all so wonderfully childish.

A client might like to imagine that his advisers are all lined up facing the same way, but banks are ferociously competitive and will do anything to score points off each other. If they're not striving to see who can cosy up closest to the company, they'll be scorning smaller rivals or rubbishing an opponent's idea and then claiming it for their own. On many occasions a company and its advisers will all be sitting around the same table, the latter grouped together in miniature tribes and radiating hostility.

43 The term 'bulge bracket' is today used to refer to any of the multinational investment banks, but it was originally coined to describe those banks whose name 'bulged' out (because of a larger font size) on the front pages of offer documents and prospectuses.

Banks aren't afraid to play dirty when it suits them. In a famous example of underhand tactics, two banks were invited over to Milan to pitch for a large investment-banking transaction. Although both were booked on the same flight out of London, one bank sent ahead a graduate trainee, got him to check in himself and a suitcase and return to the office. The rest of the team then boarded a second flight and, as they cruised up and over the Alps, their rivals sat stuck on the tarmac while frantic (and futile) efforts were made to locate the owner of the bag. Needless to say, there was only one winner of the mandate, and while nothing could be proved in the way of mischief making, the coincidence didn't pass unnoticed!

THE CITY IS a small place, and just as barristers regularly lock horns, so bankers do the same. Denigrating the competition can often work to your disadvantage – victims might be obstructive on future transactions or will bad-mouth you to companies with whom they enjoy good relationships and whom you're hoping to impress. Much of the time a banker will win a mandate and then invite his friends from other banks to join the syndicate.

Talking Tactics

Successful companies pile up profits and then wonder what to do with the money. This is where you come in. You help them spend it.

Other companies run into trouble and need to be rescued. This is also where you come in. You help bail them out.

Tactics are part and parcel of the job. At its highest level, investment banking is a real-life game of chess, with bankers as queens and company executives as sacrificial pawns. Where any deal is concerned, we can make some general observations: namely that a) bringing it to fruition is always harder than you expect, b) deals have many moving parts and so tactics vary and c) shareholders/ management teams/rival bankers all have a habit of scuppering your best-laid plans.

Most transactions are divided up into two stages: 'origination' and 'execution'. Origination can take years and is the creative side of investment banking. There's much in the way of ground preparation – analysing industries and companies, formulating ideas, gathering data, sweet-talking clients, identifying potential buyers or sellers and negotiating with the opposition. Once a deal gets approval in principal then the execution stage swings into action. This can take several months and is all about getting a deal done from a technical perspective, from processing documentation and securing shareholder approval to appeasing the various authorities and dealing with issues such as 'material adverse change' (as when markets move or economies fluctuate and deal terms have to be sweetened or soured accordingly).

§

> EXECUTING/CLOSING the deal is just as vital as winning it and most people tend to be more adept at one or the other (there are few all-rounders). For every extrovert originator an investment bank needs a technician in the engine room prepared to get his hands dirty.

Companies grow in two main ways: 'organically' (ie via their own internal momentum) and by acquisition. Acquisitions suit various parties, from executives bent on empire building to M&A bankers greedy for fees and entrepreneurs/shareholders set on selling a business to the highest bidder. If you're convincing a client to make a move for a rival business or if a client asks you for advice on a similar subject, then you'll have to consider a number of factors:[44]

a) Should the approach be friendly or hostile (ie will the target's shareholders welcome an offer or will they turn it down flat)?

A friendly approach involves a lot less stress and will help smooth your path considerably. Companies that receive unsolicited and/or unwelcome expressions of interest will fight tooth and nail to preserve their sovereignty. Imagine opening the door to a billionaire and listening as he begs you to sell him your treasured home. Would you slam the door in his face? And if you didn't how much money and/or pleading would it take before you agreed?

b) Who should be approached first – management/board or shareholders? A board will often 'recommend' a deal that shareholders then have the right to veto (although, as we have seen, they rarely do).

Investment bankers have fingers in many pies, and it might just happen that you know/can gain access to an influential board member or shareholder. Not everyone from the target company will necessarily be pulling the same way – a chief executive might have his own reasons for wanting to do a deal that a board member or leading shareholder unceremoniously rejects. It can make a big difference if you can help pave the way towards a mutually agreeable solution.

---

44 Depending on the nationality of the target, there are strict rules as to how and when the acquirer may proceed.

c) How should the acquirer convince the market/its shareholders of the benefits of the deal? Can these benefits be quantified in terms of improved positioning and cost savings?

Bankers are the most enthusiastic of salesmen and will work hard to convince everyone – from fund managers to the girl in the office canteen – of the merits of a deal. But all they see is the end result – the long hours of the night spent fudging numbers into something palatable (and turning ordinary people into disposable statistics) are how analysts and associates earn their corn.

d) Should the acquirer be open about its intentions from the outset or should it first build a stake and then make a move? Will an approach flush out other bidders and, if so, what's the most the acquirer is prepared/can afford to pay? If the deal falls apart what's the danger of other rivals moving in?

In a world of blink first and you lose, rival bankers are like latter-day gunslingers. Show your hand too quickly and you might get burned. When an asset is regarded as unique or strategically vital, bidders with deeper pockets can always emerge. Many banks lose out because they jump before they're ready and are then trampled on in the ensuing rush.

e) To what extent will the acquirer itself be vulnerable if the deal comes to naught?

There are numerous examples of companies failing to land deals and then being bid for themselves. Stick your head above the parapet only if you think it's worth your while. There's nothing more embarrassing than helping a once ambitious client to stare down the barrel of a P45.

f) How should the deal be structured? Will the acquirer offer cash, shares or other incentives? Will the acquirer need to raise extra debt or equity and who will arrange this?

Many deals don't happen or turn sour because the target doesn't like the colour of the bidder's money. Offering a bidder's shares in lieu of cash is all very well if they're seen as a desirable currency, but this is not always the case. On certain occasions it can make sense to structure a deal as a merger and not a takeover. Mergers imply different semantic considerations and can smooth over any loss of executive face – to some people the idea of being taken over is all too emasculating.

g) What should happen to the target's existing management team? Is there a place for them in the new company?

Appropriating somebody's birthright is never an easy process, especially if you're set on banishing them once a deal goes through (even if you keep them the stench of their resentment can linger on for months). Some bidders underestimate the value of the target's management and then watch in horror as employees and customers depart in droves. Ironically – because if anyone should know better, they should – this often happens when one investment bank buys another.

h) Are there tax, legal, accounting or pension issues that need to be resolved (more of an issue in cross-border transactions)? Will the deal encounter political, trade union or regulatory opposition?

People like nothing more than to kick up a fuss when sovereignty, jobs and market share are all at stake, and investment banks have many ways to smooth things over.

Some banks have internal legal departments that could even rival what some of the so-called 'magic circle' firms have to boast.

Of course, the target and its advisers will be weighing up these same (and other) issues from their side of the fence:

a) Is this the right time in the company's development to join forces with a larger entity or should it continue to go it alone? Do shareholders need/want to sell? What will be the commercial repercussions if they say no?

Some companies come to the natural end of their independent lives and begin to cast the net for suitors. Indeed many entrepreneurs start businesses with the express intention of selling them several years later. Any number of dot-com fantasists used to say (with a straight face), 'I'm going to sell this business before it gets too big.'

b) Is the acquirer their partner of choice or would they prefer to get into bed with somebody else (known in financial parlance as a 'white knight')?

Just as not every girl gets to dance with the love of her life so not every company attracts the bidder it wants. Target companies and their bankers are quick to sound out other suitors if they think their independence is under threat.

c) What do shareholders think their company is worth and what deal terms/price are they prepared to accept?

If shareholders decide it's time to sell then they'll want to hold out for the highest possible price, as flushing out rival bidders can only be to their advantage. Bankers prefer disposals – trying to buy something is always fraught with uncertainty, especially when you're dealing with rival bidders and an unwilling seller, whereas conducting a 'beauty parade' is far less risky – you have an asset to sell and must find the highest bidder/most suitable fit.

There is, of course, no guarantee you'll be successful. No one might be prepared to meet the seller's price, markets might lurch in violent, unexpected directions and boards and/or management teams might suddenly pull the plug, piqued by what they deem to be derisory offers or unsatisfactory deal terms.

NEVER MIND THE hot money that investors pump into possible bid targets, the days following a bid announcement are feast days for buy and sell side alike. Hedge funds will stake massive bets (in a strategy known as 'merger arbitrage') on the chances of bidder A raising its bid for B or on the likely appearance of bidder C. Shareholder registers can be transformed with bewildering speed as hedge funds march in and the long-only fraternity cut and run, with broking firms sitting in the middle and salivating as the commission flows in. Assessing the probability of a deal going through or of other bidders emerging is an analytical industry in itself – when markets are booming whole departments will be given over to this activity.

Flashing the Cash

If in the last section we concentrated on the advisory side of things, the arrangement and the provision of financing is an equally vital cog in the investment-banking machine. Most transactions involve the raising of capital in some form or another, and this is where the capital-markets function of a bank comes into play, helping a client structure/organise its requirements and liaising with investors (be they banks, governments, pension funds, hedge funds or individuals).

As capital markets is both client and market facing, its protagonists work with everyone – companies, bankers, corporate brokers, analysts, traders, salesmen, investors, lawyers, accountants and compliance departments – and provide much of the process behind (such as checking and producing the endless documentation) and the organisation of transactions ranging from bond issuance to rights issues and IPOs.[45]

CAPITAL MARKETS DEPARTMENTS also get involved with large secondary transactions, conducting 'book builds' (ie building a book of investors) for shareholders looking to sell sizeable stakes in a company. A favourite hedge-fund trick is to a) get wind of a placing (thanks to porous Chinese Walls), b) go short the stock and c) buy it back in the placing. In order to encourage investors to take part, most placings are done at a discount to the current share price, and this way the hedge fund sells the stock at a higher price than it buys it, thereby booking a profit. Back in 2003–07 investment banks were crawling with hedge-fund spies – some funds had an uncanny knack of knowing exactly when a placing would be announced.

If a client wishes to raise money, a capital-markets department will help it decide how much capital it requires, in what form and at what price, having some-

45 Indeed, it's so central that in most firms capital-markets departments are located in fishtank-type boxes on the dealing floor (and not shut off from the world with the rest of corporate finance). Because of the need to maintain Chinese Walls bankers can come out but brokers, analysts, etc, aren't allowed in.

times first contacted potential investors and canvassed their views. Although they often do this in tandem with the bank's debt or equity sales forces, bankers also have a direct line to the most important investors. Having market feel or an ear to the ground can be vital when trying to establish which way the wind is blowing.

This doesn't mean they always get it right. Many capital-markets people are bankers and not brokers by trade, and as a consequence feel that their loyalties lie with the company and not the investor. Many IPOs fall apart or have to be revised because bankers promise companies the earth in terms of price and/or financial incentives, discover that the sales team can't get the deal done and then refuse to compromise. It's not uncommon to see bankers and brokers both at each other's throats, each complaining that the other is a waste of time and/or doesn't have a clue what he's talking about. As we have already mentioned, rare is the man who can empathise with every perspective. More often than not he's a broker-turned-banker. Traffic hardly ever flows in the other direction. Why would a banker demean himself so?

IF YOU ASKED a broker why so few bankers cross the divide and become brokers you'd receive a very different response. A common perception of bankers, especially those in capital-markets departments, is that they are intellectually overbearing and have little in the way of people skills.

Capital-markets transactions are as hierarchical, and hence as snobbish, as any. We have already seen in an earlier chapter (see *Equity Sales*) how the syndicate structure functions where primary business/capital raising is concerned, but it's worth pointing out that, as with advisory mandates, firms will a) do anything to get on the ticket even if they offer next to nothing and b) fight tooth and nail to have their name as prominently placed as possible on the documentation (known as a 'prospectus' for an IPO). In a capital-markets transaction a 'book runner' is the advisory equivalent of a 'lead' and the hierarchy runs all the way down to a 'co-manager' at the bottom. The book runner decides everything, from which investors receive the stock to which get a 'one-on-one' meeting with the company management. A co-manager will be lucky if his clients are laid a place at a group lunch meeting.

When helping a client raise capital a bank will often 'underwrite' the issue, in other words provide a promise that it will stump up the money in the event it fails to raise it from the market. Underwriting fees tend to be icing on the cake/another way of fleecing the client – banks won't underwrite deals unless they are confident of finding the capital, and in most cases will have already received the necessary assurances from the investment community.

$

BANKS CAN SOMETIMES get overconfident. In the summer of 2007 they were underwriting large slugs of private equity/leveraged buy-out debt that they couldn't sell on when the music stopped, and were left with colossal amounts of unwanted paper (debt) on their hands (the £11.1bn takeover of Alliance Boots, a transaction that marked the peak of the European private equity boom, is just one such example). Other banks love it when a rival comes unstuck and will attempt to prolong the agony in any way possible (such as making sure everyone else knows or bashing the asset the rival is holding).

Dark Arts

Investment bankers love to think they're men of substance, a breed of über intellects, and within most banks there are teams who specialise in dreaming up structures and instruments beyond the ken of the average man (and unfortunately the average banker).

For years banks harboured and nurtured the rocket scientists behind the credit derivatives that would later bring the world's banking system to its knees. We can point the finger now, but back then banks were too busy pocketing fees to appreciate the perils of their more covert operations. These bankers were arranging structures and selling products that worked on one premise and one premise alone: that all would be well as long as economies continued to prosper. And when the bubble burst, triggered by people no one had ever heard of in parts of the United States no one had ever visited, the world (and its bankers) suddenly woke up to the fact that sub-prime mortgage default was not a problem confined to American trailer parks.

'Securitisation' is just one example of a clever financing structure and is related to hedge funds, private equity, leveraged buy-outs, share buy-backs, etc, in that it is another branch of the recently discredited credit tree. It's a sophisticated name for collaterised lending, ie borrowing money against the future cash you expect your assets to generate. In the pre-crunch days lenders attached all manner of punitive criteria that banks waved through, convincing their clients (the borrowers) that nothing could go wrong. But when the meteor struck, companies that had put up bricks, mortar and any other cash-generating asset as collateral suddenly found themselves locked out of their properties and hounded off their land, their appeals for clemency falling on the deafest of ears.

Real estate-backed companies that had moved assets into ring-fenced vehicles against which they borrowed were particularly badly hit. As economies slowed and tenants struggled to pay their rent or renew their leases these assets fell into the hands of lenders. The companies complained to their bankers but in vain – the small print demanded that if a minimum rental level was not achieved then the original owner would forfeit the right to the asset.

Let's not be naïve – bubbles will come and go and banks will continue to dupe their clients into intricate, incomprehensible schemes (that the authorities will be slow to police). When people are making money they never worry about the small print. That's the nature of capitalism.

Loose Tongues

In the City the fact that information is leaked is no surprise, especially in corporate finance. However much people might like to believe in a code of *omertà* or in the impenetrability of Chinese Walls, when one stops to consider just how much manpower is needed for the average transaction it's incredible just how many deals remain beneath the radar. So many people are in the loop – bankers, corporate brokers, company executives, board members, lawyers, accountants, public-relations officers, printers, wives and secretaries to name but several – that a leak can spring from anywhere. You only need someone with a lack of scruples and/or discretion or with an agenda to let the cat out of the bag.

Let's now have a look at some of the ways in which/ reasons why information escapes the net:

a) Feeding the media frenzy.

Just as politicians play the media to their advantage, so workers in the City do the same. Having a prominent journalist as an unofficial mouthpiece is a luxury enjoyed by more people than you might imagine, from bankers/companies/individuals wishing to leak/scupper deals to fund managers wanting to talk up an investment.

Sometimes journalists seem just too well informed. It's incredible just how often the business sections of the press get it right when they lead with yet another sensational splash.

'Tomorrow X will announce the acquisition of Y for $60 a share. The deal has been agreed between the two boards and will create an industry behemoth. X is represented by UBS and JP Morgan and Y by Morgan Stanley and Credit Suisse.'

Or

'On Thursday RWE will announce Q1 results that will beat market expectations.'

Or

'Cosmic Caravans has been in discussions with its advisers and leading shareholders and will next week announce a deeply discounted rights issue at $1 a share.'

A journalist can be employed for any number of reasons. In an M&A deal the acquirer's advisers might want him to paint a deal in a favourable light, the sellers may want to flush out other bidders or someone with a vested interest (such as a member of management or the board) may want to scupper the deal. Having the media onside can also bolster a company's fortunes in the run-up to an important results announcement. For some strange reason investors are more likely to believe 'objective' journalists than they are public-relations spin doctors, or even the company itself.

b) Idle chatter

People love to talk and to speculate, and the City adores gossip and rumour mongering.

'Have you heard? Amanda's husband has been to India on business twice in the last week.'

'Doesn't he work for Citigroup and specialise in food retail M&A?'

'That's right. Do you think they're lining up a bid for you know who?'

c) Souls of indiscretion

Some people struggle to keep their mouths shut, especially if they have a taste for alcohol:

'I know I shouldn't tell you this, but my brother's been working on a massive deal for the past few months in Greece. One of his clients is going to bid for a Greek bank. Yes, thanks, I'd love another pint.'

Or,

'Our corporate guys are working on a rights issue for one of the cement producers. It shouldn't take a genius to work out which one – we're being linked to them all the time.'

People often forget that in most jurisdictions the law states that even if you do not benefit yourself, the act of telling someone something 'inside' is tantamount to criminality. Proving that you said it is, of course, another issue altogether.

Bonus Behaviour

Investment bankers are no less fixated on remuneration than their peers on the other side of the Chinese Walls, and the tricks they employ to ensure they get what (they feel) they deserve are florid to say the least. Bankers are among the City's highest earners and get paid in a similar way to brokers, traders and analysts in that they receive a bonus (in cash and shares) in addition to their basic salary.

In the run-up to bonus/review season (which is October–December in most firms), it's common for bankers to undergo some form of personality transplant. Individuals renowned for their cruelty and/or lack of vigour will be suddenly transformed into energetic Florence Nightingales, reminding their bosses on an almost hourly basis of how many deals they've been involved in (however tenuously) that year and showering their juniors with platitudes and blandishments. Many firms operate what is known as the '360-degree review system' where every employee, however lowly, is invited to give their (anonymous) opinions of each and every colleague. A bad mark can have serious implications for your prospects of promotion (and hence of pay).

During this time departments that were moribund will overnight become hives of activity. Transaction pipelines will be miraculously reinvigorated and bankers will predict to anyone who'll listen the prospect of bumper fees tomorrow (ie after this year's bonuses have been paid). Speculation will be rife as to the likely size of the pool, with weekly updates being leaked from on high as management tries to 'manage down expectations'.

Just as for those on the other side of the Chinese Walls, bonus pools depend in part on how different departments have performed. While most people will never be happy and will rant and rave, management will look for every excuse to trim you down to what they believe is the level needed to retain you (and not a penny more). In most firms the bonus pool is a carefully calibrated number based on retention requirements, and human-resources departments are quite happy to consult their peers at rival firms in an attempt to set a benchmark.

While management will conspire to toe the party line where their subordinates are concerned, they're not averse to kicking each other in the teeth. Some managing directors who don't deliver the goods will find their way onto remuneration committees as a means of self-preservation, and will claim the credit for deals in which they have had no or little involvement. Others will feel a patronising hand on their shoulder and be informed (discreetly, of course) that they have six months to phase themselves out. This is a world of short contract duration and closely monitored performance metrics. Those that sit on their laurels don't last the course.

§ ───────────

> THERE IS SUCH a thing as the 'bonus hangover'. After the cascade of adrenaline that precedes 'D Day', you can suffer from the most almighty withdrawal symptoms once you find out your fate, especially if your better half has already frittered away a large proportion of the cash on a new kitchen and a Caribbean holiday with her parents. The road ahead to next year's fix will suddenly look very long and very rocky.

Conclusion

Not for nothing do investment bankers regard themselves as the titans of the capitalist world. They drive the bandwagon and others follow in their wake. If companies didn't raise money, acquire each other or list on stock markets, brokers and traders would have nothing to trade, analysts nothing to analyse and fund managers nothing to buy or sell. If anyone earns their money it is most definitely them, or so they'd have you believe.

Reaching the investment-banking summit is no joke – it's a marathon for insomniacs. You'll be taken from your comfort zone, drowned in a sea of spreadsheets, late nights and social deprivation and released into a world you don't recognise, rich, 30 but going on 50. A corporate financier must have brains and brawn.

But once you hit the peak you mustn't stop and admire the view. The intellectual high ground may look stunning, but those who stand still freeze to death. The successful banker never rests, combining creativity with obduracy and social flair with political nous.

This is not a land where the young bucks rule – grey hair, experience and sagacity predominate. The King is dead. Long live the King! But patriarchs don't always lead by example and bankers ride high in a cast list of credit-crunch villains. Short-termism is the City swine flu and some bankers have it bad. Bag fees first, ask questions later, is an all too common refrain.